# Better Homes and Gardens.

# CHRISTMAS JOYS

## T·O C·R·A·F·T & S·T·I·T·C·H

© Copyright 1985 by Meredith Corporation, Des Moines, Iowa.
All Rights Reserved. Printed in the United States of America.
First Edition. First Printing.
Library of Congress Catalog Card Number: 84-62405
ISBN: 0-696-01430-0 (hard cover)
ISBN: 0-696-01432-7 (trade paperback)

## BETTER HOMES AND GARDENS. BOOKS

Editor: Gerald M. Knox
Art Director: Ernest Shelton
Managing Editor: David A. Kirchner

Crafts Editor: Nancy Lindemeyer
Senior Crafts Books Editor: Joan Cravens
Associate Crafts Books Editors: Laura Holtorf Collins,
   Rebecca Jerdee, Sara Jane Treinen

Associate Art Directors: Linda Ford Vermie,
   Neoma Alt West, Randall Yontz
Copy and Production Editors: Marsha Jahns,
   Mary Helen Schiltz, Carl Voss, David A. Walsh
Assistant Art Directors: Lynda Haupert,
   Harijs Priekulis, Tom Wegner
Senior Graphic Designers: Mike Eagleton,
   Lyne Neymeyer
Graphic Designers: Mike Burns, Sally Cooper,
   Stan Sams, Darla Whipple-Frain

Vice President, Editorial Director: Doris Eby
Executive Director, Editorial Services: Duane Gregg

General Manager: Fred Stines
Director of Publishing: Robert B. Nelson
Vice President, Retail Marketing: Jamie Martin
Vice President, Direct Marketing: Arthur Heydendael

**Christmas Joys To Craft and Stitch**
Crafts Editor: Laura Holtorf Collins
Contributing Editor: James A. Williams
Copy and Production Editor: David A. Walsh
Graphic Designer: D. Greg Thompson
Contributing Designers: Alisann Dixon, Randall Yontz,
   Lyne Neymeyer
Electronic Text Processor: Donna Russell

# CONTENTS

Craft a Merry Christmas ———————— 4

Baked clay ornaments   4
Crocheted treetop angel   6
Cameo rose ornaments   7
Crocheted snowflake ornaments   7
Crocheted cornucopia centerpiece and party favors   8
Crepe paper angel   9
Crepe paper wreath   10
Patchwork nativity   12

Enchanting Christmas Needlecrafts
Needlepoint Poinsettia Wreath ————— 24

Celebrate with Red and Green ———— 30

Smocked ornaments, pinafores, and wreath   30
Crazy quilt stocking and ornaments   34
Quick-and-easy Christmas stocking, ornaments, and wreath   35
Appliquéd guest towels   36
Christmas tree place mats   36
Pieced and quilted table runner   37
Patchwork tablecloth   38
Lath barn landscape   39
Homespun doll   39

Enchanting Christmas Needlecrafts
Cross-Stitched Sampler ——————— 48

Holiday Treats for Children ————— 54

Tin soldier ornaments   55
Child's knitted silent night vest   56
Child's embroidered snow scene jumper   57
Three appliquéd Christmas stockings   58
Santa doll and reindeer toy   59
Painted and embroidered angel wall hanging and
   ornaments   60
Cross-stitched Christmas stocking   61
Festive cross-stitched skirt   62
Tabletop Advent tree   63

Enchanting Christmas Needlecrafts
Crocheted Gingerbread House ————— 74

Acknowledgments ———————————— 80

# Craft a Merry Christmas

Christmas is a special time. The magic and wonder of stories told, the fond remembrance of holidays past, and the excitement of the current festivities draw family and friends together. A loving and thoughtful way to celebrate the season is with handcrafted gifts, trims, and treasures.

This year craft a merry Christmas using a variety of techniques. On the next few pages you'll find crocheted decorations and ornaments, a patchwork nativity, an elegant "corn husk" wreath and angel, as well as the delightful bread dough ornaments, *left*.

Fanciful maidens, geese, and lambs adorn packages and hang from evergreen boughs, bringing cheer to one and all. Instructions are given for the goose, kneeling lamb, and girl with an apron full of hearts. Use these instructions and the photograph to craft other trim ideas. Instructions for all projects in this section begin on page 14.

# CRAFT A MERRY CHRISTMAS

Crochet is a popular technique with needle artists today. On these and the next two pages, you'll find all kinds of wonderful home accessories, gifts, and decorations to help make your holidays brighter.

The delightful angel, *opposite,* is a unique example of this technique. Simple stitches crocheted in a repeat pattern form the lacy gown. Single crochet, worked around a plastic foam egg, creates the head. An open mesh pattern with scalloped edging fashions the wings, and metallic threads highlight the wings, collar, and halo.

Stiffened with glue, she's a perfect treetop ornament or mantel decoration for elegant holiday occasions.

Exquisite cameo crochet ornaments, *left,* add a delicate accent to your holiday tree.

Although filet crochet works up easily in a single color—and these ornaments would be lovely in just one shade—experienced crocheters will enjoy the challenge of cameo crochet, which uses two or more colors.

Work a long strip of pink flowers and green leaves against a white mesh background. Then, stiffen this "yardage" using a mixture of glue and water. Cut out hearts or other cookie-cutter shapes and finish with lace and satin bows.

Pastel shades of cotton thread add glamour to the snowflakes, *right.*

Display these fanciful ornaments on your tree, showcase them on a holiday gift of flowers (as shown here), or suspend a "blizzardful" in a window.

Make them by the dozens to trim special packages, give as last-minute gifts, or sell at holiday bazaars.

# CRAFT A MERRY CHRISTMAS

**E**xquisite cornucopias in crisp white crochet are enticing examples of the crocheter's art. Basic stitches combine to create these unusual decorations. They make great bazaar items and gifts, but you're sure to want some for your home, too.

The cornucopia centerpiece, *at left, above,* makes a striking table decoration for elegant holiday teas or special occasions any time of the year. A lacy border with scalloped edging drapes softly and accents a spray of evergreens and flowers.

**S**maller versions of the elegant cornucopia are bedecked with ribbon and serve as enchanting party favors, *at left, below,* or as lacy tree trims, *above.*

On your Christmas tree, a single cornucopia makes a special ornament that will hold a secret present for someone you love.

Or fill a tree full of the lacy, Victorian-inspired ornaments. And, as in Victorian times, fill the cornucopias with tiny treats and candies for the children, or fashion small silk flower bouquets to tuck inside each ornament.

For a Christmastime tea party, fill each take-home favor with a small gift and peppermints or other wrapped candies. The honored guests are sure to treasure their handcrafted mementos.

# CRAFT A MERRY CHRISTMAS

The everlasting floral wreath, *opposite*, has a special charm that makes it an unusual Christmas decoration. Delicate and graceful, it's just too pretty to put away after the holiday season.

Use it year-round as a trim for a doorway, mantel top, or table centerpiece.

To make the wreath, cut and form the buds and flowers from painted crepe paper and purchased stamens.

Arrange the lavish blooms and crepe paper leaves around a wire wreath frame, using dried baby's breath as a filler. Small flowers and curly vines add textural interest and visual detail.

Carry this exquisite theme to your Christmas tree, if you like, by making dozens of pretty paper blossoms and wiring them to the evergreen boughs. Then, fill in the tree with bouquets of baby's breath and garlands of the smaller vine flowers to create a breathtaking, country-fresh Christmas.

Corn husk flowers and dolls, made by early settlers as simple decorations and toys, take on a sophisticated look when fashioned from sturdy crepe paper painted in pastel hues.

A heavenly crepe paper angel, pictured *at right*, is crafted in delicate shades of pink and recalls the corn husk dolls of long ago.

Simple shaping of the crepe paper forms the gentle folds and curls of the angel's wings and gown. Flowing hair and a delicate bouquet add detail.

Whether you use the doll as a centerpiece for a Christmas Eve dinner table or place her atop a glorious tree, you'll find this angel a lovely addition to your family's holiday traditions.

2.99

# CRAFT A MERRY CHRISTMAS

A nativity scene is a wonderful way to teach and tell the Christmas story. Use the traditional art of patchwork to create this delightful setting, piecing the figures by hand or machine for a unique application of this popular craft technique.

These pieced and embroidered figures will become a favorite part of your children's Christmas celebration. And the adorable patchwork donkey, *below* and *right,* can double as a toy for a deserving youngster.

The 12-inch-tall figures are crafted from scraps of muslin, calico, and wool with bits of ribbon, lace trims, and braid for embellishment and detail.

Craft Mary and Joseph, *opposite,* from colorful pieces of prints and solids. Joseph's robe is made from tiny squares. Mary and the Infant wear patchwork of tiny prints. Embroidered facial features, delicate trims, and halos embellish the figures.

Fashion the kneeling shepherd, *below,* from scraps of burlap and neutral-tone fabrics with embroidered beard and features. Make sheep, *opposite,* from a nubby knit. Craft the cradle from twigs and wisps of excelsior.

After you've made the figures shown, you'll want to create more to enlarge the scene. Work three kings using the patterns for Joseph and the shepherd.

Use elegant silks, brocades, and velvets for their costumes and embroider with gold and silver. Fashion their crowns from tiny seed pearls and beads.

# CRAFT A MERRY CHRISTMAS

## Baked-Clay Ornaments

Shown on pages 4–5.

**MATERIALS**
Flour, salt, and water (clay)
Paste food coloring (available at cake decorating stores)
White acrylic paint
Garlic press; miniature heart and flower cutters (available at miniature shops)
Bugle beads (eyes); paraffin
Cookie sheet; plastic bags; knives; plastic wrap; foil; paper clips; side cutters; straw; spatula; and pinking shears

**INSTRUCTIONS**

**Clay recipe (for 6–8 ornaments)**
Mix 1 cup *each* of salt and water, and 2 cups of flour. The consistency of the clay should be fairly stiff; add extra water or flour as needed.
Mix small amounts of food coloring into *natural-color* dough to achieve desired shades. (Mix pink and brown together for flesh color.) Use white acrylic paint for white (or leave clay its natural color). Store clay in plastic bags.
When rolling dough for flat shapes, roll to ⅛-inch thickness.

**Lamb**
Use white dough for lamb, except use pink for ears and assorted color(s) for bow or flowers.

BODY: Break off a piece of dough about the size of a baby food jar lid. Roll into a ball, then roll into a teardrop shape about 1 inch in diameter at widest point and 3¼ inches long (narrow end becomes neck). Turn up narrow end of teardrop shape for neck. Set body aside on clean surface. (The back of the body should lie flat on the surface.)

HEAD: Break off a piece of dough the size of a quarter; roll into a ball. Form nose at one end of ball, pulling out dough about ⅜ inch; place on neck of lamb body. Push two black bugle beads into head for eyes. Using a knife, pierce Y shape to define nose.

EARS: Roll out two teardrop shapes about ½ inch long (⅜ inch wide at widest point). Flatten slightly. Dampen the sides of the head and press ears in place.

LEGS: For hind leg, roll out a coil, 1¾ inches long, leaving one end larger (about ¾ inch in diameter). Press large end to back of body; turn narrow end toward front of lamb.
For front legs, roll out a ⅜-inch-diameter coil, 3 inches long; cut in half. Press foreleg atop back leg (position the foreleg to the right of the back leg). Bend legs toward hind leg.

TAIL: Press on small oval.

FLEECE: Using a garlic press, squeeze out dough ⅛ inch long at a time; cut off. Moisten the head slightly; lightly press cut dough around face. Repeat for body (see photograph for placement).
Cut a paper clip in half using side cutters. Insert half of paper clip into body back for hanging.

LAMB TRIMS: Roll out colored dough for flowers. Cut out with a miniature cutter; position around neck. Or, cut a ¼-inch-wide strip from dough; fashion into a bow.

FINISHING: Using a spatula, lift finished ornament onto a foil-lined cookie sheet. Bake at 325° for several hours until hard.
Melt paraffin in a double boiler and dip ornament into paraffin.

**Goose**
Use white dough for body, yellow for beak and feet, and assorted colors for flowers or ribbons.

BODY: Break off a piece of the dough and roll into a ball 1½ inches in diameter. Roll one end, elongating it 2 inches for neck. Pinch opposite end to form tail.

NECK AND HEAD: Turn up elongated end to form neck and head; poke a hole into elongated end for beak insertion. Roll small oval from yellow for beak. Insert into hole; pinch beak to flatten. Insert bead eye.

FEET: Roll two small ovals for feet, leaving bottom ends of ovals wider for feet; turn up wide ends to form feet. Press in place.

WING: Roll out a pointed oval for wing; flatten and score one side for feather detail. Press onto body. Insert paper clip hanger.

GOOSE TRIMS: Make flowers or ribbon streamers as directed for lamb. Fashion ribbon into a bow, or hang ribbons from beak.

FINISHING: Finish as directed above for lamb.

**Girl with apron full of hearts**
Mix dough as follows: white for apron and feet; peach for dress;

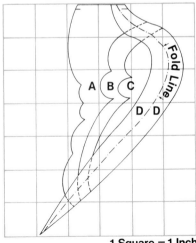

1 Square = 1 Inch

flesh for face and hands; pink for cheeks; yellow for hair; blue for hair bow; and assorted colors for hearts.

DRESS: Roll out peach dough; cut a 3x8-inch rectangle (skirt) and a 1-inch square (bodice).

Place bodice on working surface. To gather dress, push dough into folds by lifting right side, gathering from right to left. Pinch away excess dough at top of skirt to fit bodice. Press skirt to bodice.

Cover with plastic wrap to prevent drying.

APRON: Roll out white dough; cut a 2x4-inch rectangle (apron skirt) and a ¾x1-inch piece (bib) using pinking shears.

Press bib to bodice. Gather 2x4-inch rectangle and press to bib. Score along top edge to simulate gathers. Fold up apron at bottom edge so it will hold hearts.

Using pinking shears, cut an oval from white dough, to measure 2 inches long and ½ inch wide at the widest part (apron straps). Cut oval in half lengthwise. Gather straight edge; press to bib front and bodice back.

ARMS: Using peach dough, roll out a ¼-inch-diameter coil, 3½ inches long; cut in half. Using a pencil, poke a hole in one end of each arm (as for goose head/beak assembly). Round off and smooth other ends for shoulders.

Roll two ovals from flesh-color dough for hands. Moisten holes in arms; press hands into holes.

Press shoulder ends to sides of bodice. Bend arms at the elbows, placing hands at sides of apron.

HEAD: Roll flesh-color dough into an oval about the size of a large olive. Press a small piece of yellow dough onto top of dress; place head on this piece.

Insert bugle beads for eyes. Cut a tiny ball of pink dough in half

for the cheeks; roll each half into balls and press onto face. Use a straw to press a grin on face.

HAIR: Using a garlic press, squeeze out about 3- to 4-inch lengths of yellow dough. Press lightly on top of head, twirling and winding lengths into desired hair style. Insert hook into top of head (see instructions for lamb to make hook). Cut out a ⅛-inch-wide strip from blue dough. Fashion into a bow; press onto hair.

HEARTS: Roll out dough in assorted colors. Using a miniature cutter, cut out enough to fill apron. Press hearts onto apron. Press one heart onto bib.

FEET: From white dough, roll a ¼-inch-diameter coil 4 inches long. Cut in half; turn ends up and flatten tips of feet to widen. Press together. Lift bottom of dress; place legs under dress using a spatula. Press dress to legs.

FINISHING: Finish as directed for lamb ornament.

# Crocheted Snowflakes

Shown on page 7.

## MATERIALS
DMC Cébélia cotton thread in assorted colors, Size 30
Size 8 steel crochet hook
Glue; rustproof pins
Aluminum foil; cardboard

**Abbreviations:** See page 53.

## INSTRUCTIONS

### Yellow snowflake
Finished size is 4½ inches in diameter. Ch 7, join with sl st for ring. *Rnd 1:* Ch 1, 12 sc in ring, join to 1st sc. *Rnd 2:* * Ch 16, sl st in 7th ch from beg and in next 6 ch, sc in same st at base of ch; sc in next st, ch 30, sl st in 7th ch from beg; (ch 24, sl st in 3rd ch from beg) twice; sl st in next 2 ch; ch 22, sl st in beg ch, sl st in next 2 ch of main stem; ch 24, sl st in

beg ch, sl st in each ch to base of stem, sc in same st, sc in next st; rep from * 5 times more; join to 1st sc. Fasten off.

**Stiffening and finishing**
Cover a piece of cardboard with aluminum foil.

Mix glue and water together in equal parts, adding just a little more water to the solution. Dip snowflake into solution, squeeze out excess glue, and stretch onto cardboard, pinning in place. Allow to dry thoroughly, remove pins, and attach monofilament thread or ribbon for hanging.

**Rose snowflake**
Finished size is 4 inches in diameter. Ch 5, join with sl st for ring. *Rnd 1:* Ch 3, 11 dc in ring, join with sl st to top of ch-3. *Rnd 2:* Sl st in sp bet beg ch and next dc, * ch 4, trc in next sp bet last dc and next dc, ch 4, sc in next sp bet last dc and next dc; rep from *; end ch 4, join to base of beg ch—6 points. *Rnd 3:* Sl st in each ch to 1st trc, sc in trc, * ch 10, sc in next trc; rep from *; join with sc in 1st sc. *Rnd 4:* * Working following ch lengths, ending each length with a sl st in beg ch: ch 18, 12, 20, 12, 18; sc in same sc at base, in next ch-10 sp work (6 sc, ch 5, 6 sc), sc in sc; rep from *; join to first sc. Fasten off. Finish as directed for yellow snowflake.

**Lavender snowflake**
Finished size is 4¼ inches in diameter. Ch 8, join with sl st for ring. *Rnd 1:* Ch 1, 18 sc in ring, join to 1st sc. *Rnd 2:* * Ch 12, sl st in same sp; ch 12, sl st in 5th ch from hook; then work following ch lengths ending each length with a sl st in beg of ch for lp: ch
*continued*

10, 5, 10, 5, 16, 5, 10, 5, 10, 5; then sl st in base of 1st ch-5 lp and in each ch along stem to base; ch 12, sl st in base, sl st in next 3 sc; rep from *, ending with sl st in rem sc, join. Fasten off.

To finish, see instructions for yellow snowflake, page 15.

### Blue snowflake

Finished size is 5¼ inches in diameter.

Ch 8, join with sl st for ring. *Rnd 1:* Ch 3, 17 dc in ring, join to top of beg ch-3. *Rnd 2:* Ch 1, sc in joining, * ch 8, sk 2 dc, sc in next dc; rep from *, join to 1st sc. *Rnd 3:* Ch 1, 10 sc in each ch-8 sp, join to 1st sc. *Rnd 4:* Work following ch lengths, ending each length with a sl st in 4th ch from beg: ch 18, 16, 14, 12, 12, 12, 14, 16, 18; ch 3, sc in base; (ch 7, sl st in 4th ch from hook) 5 times; ch 3, sk next 9 sc, sc in next sc; rep from *, ending with ch 3, sk 9 sc, join to beg ch. Fasten off.

To finish, see instructions for yellow snowflake, page 15.

# Crocheted Angel

Shown on page 6.

Finished size is 11 inches tall.

### MATERIALS
2 balls of white DMC Cébélia cotton thread, Size 20
Metallic gold thread
Size 8 steel crochet hook
Plastic egg for head
Yarn for hair
12-inch length brass wire

**Abbreviations:** See page 53.

### INSTRUCTIONS
Beg at neck edge, ch 10, join with sl st to make ring.

*Rnd 1:* Ch 1, sc in same st as join and in each ch around; join to 1st sc.

*Rnd 2:* Ch 1, sc in same st as join and in each sc around; join to 1st sc. *Rnds 3-4:* Rep Rnd 2.

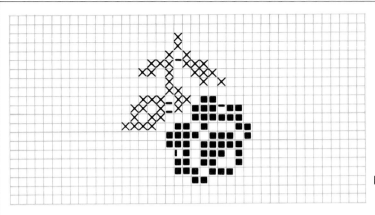

ROW 10

DRESS: *Rnd 5:* Ch 3, dc in same st as join, 2 dc in each sc around; join to top of ch-3—20 dc counting beg ch-3 as dc.

*Rnd 6:* Ch 3, dc in same st as join; * ch 1, sk dc, 2 dc in next dc; rep from * around; join last ch-1 to top of ch-3.

*Rnd 7:* Ch 3, dc in next dc; * in ch-1 sp work sc, 2 dc, sc; dc in each of next 2 dc; rep from * around; join to top of ch-3. *Rnd 8:* Sl st in next 2 sts; ch 1, sc in same st as last sl st; * ch 3, sk 2 dc, sc in next sc; rep from * around; join last ch-3 to sc at beg of rnd.

*Rnd 9:* Sl st in next ch-3 sp, ch 1, in same sp work (sc, 2 dc, trc, ch 1, trc, 2 dc, sc). * In next ch-3 sp work (sc, 2 dc, trc, ch 1, trc, 2 dc, sc); rep from * around; join to 1st sc—20 scallops made.

*Rnd 10:* Sl st in next 3 sts and ch-1 sp; ch 1, sc in same sp; * ch 5, sc in ch-1 sp of next scallop; rep from * around; join last ch-5 to sc at beg of rnd.

*Rnd 11:* Sl st in ch-5 lp, ch 3, in same lp work (2 dc, ch 1, 3 dc); * sk next 5 ch-5 lps, (in next ch-5 lp work 3 dc, ch 2, 3 dc) 5 times; rep from * once more; except rep bet ( )'s 4 times; join to top of ch-3.

*Rnd 12:* Ch 3, dc in next 2 dc; * dc in ch-1 sp; dc in next 6 dc; rep from * around; end dc in last 3 dc; join to top of ch-3—70 sts.

*Rnd 13:* Ch 3, dec over next 2 dc as follows: *(yo, draw up lp in next dc, yo, draw through 2 lps on hook) twice; yo, draw through 3 lps on hook—dec made.* * Dc in next 3 dc, dec over next 2 dc; dc in next dc, dec over next 2 dc; rep from * around, ending dec over

last 2 dc; join to top of ch-3—53 sts.

*Rnd 14:* Ch 3, dc in each dc around, *and at the same time,* dec 13 sts evenly spaced; join to top of ch-3—40 sts.

*Rnds 15–17:* Ch 1, sc in same st as join; sc in each st around; join to 1st sc.

*Rnd 18:* Ch 3, dc in same st as join, 2 dc in each sc around; join to top of ch-3—80 dc.

*Rnd 19:* Ch 1, sc in same st as join; * ch 3, sk 2 dc, sc in next dc; rep from * around; join last ch-3 to 1st sc.

*Rnd 20:* Rep Rnd 9—27 scallops made. *Rnd 21:* Rep Rnd 10. *Rnd 22:* In each ch-5 lp around work 8 sc; join to 1st sc.

*Rnd 23:* Ch 5, sk 2 sc, dc in next sc; * ch 2, sk 2 sc, dc in next sc; rep from * around; join to 3rd ch of ch-5—72 ch-2 lps.

*Rnd 24:* Sl st in next ch-lp, ch 3, 2 dc in same lp, ch 3, 3 dc in same lp; * sk next ch-lp; in next ch-lp work 3 dc, ch 3, 3 dc; rep from * around; join to top of ch-3.

*Rnd 25:* Sl st in next 2 dc and ch-3 sp; ch 3, 6 dc in same ch-3 lp; * 7 dc in next ch-3 sp; rep from * around; join to top of ch-3.

*Rnd 26:* Sl st in next 3 dc, ch 1, sc in same st as last sl st; * ch 5, sc in center dc on next scallop; rep from * around; join last ch-5 to 1st sc. *Rnd 27:* Rep Rnd 22.

*Rnd 28:* Ch 5, sk 3 sc, dc in next sc; * ch 2, sk 3 sc, dc in next sc, rep from * around; join last ch-2 to 3rd ch of ch-5.

*Rnds 29-31:* Rep Rnds 24-26. *Rnd 32:* Rep Rnd 22. *Rnd 33:* Rep Rnd 28. Rep Rnds 29-33 three more times; rep Rnds 24 and 25. Fasten off.

SLEEVE: Join thread in any ch-5 lp at armhole edge and work 8 sc in each 7 lps around armhole, join to 1st sc.

*Rnd 1:* Rep Rnd 23. *Rnd 2:* Rep Rnd 24. *Rnd 3:* Rep Rnd 25. *Rnd 4:* Rep Rnd 26. *Rnd 5:* Rep Rnd 22. Rep Rnds 2-5 once more, then rep Rnds 2, 3, and 4.

*Rnd 13:* Sl st in next 3 dc, ch 1, sc in same st as join; * ch 2, sc in center dc of next scallop, rep from * around; join to 1st sc.

*Rnd 14:* Work 2 sc in each ch-2 lp around. *Rnd 15:* Sc in each sc around. Fasten off. Rep sleeve for other armhole.

WING (make 2): Ch 8, join to form ring. *Row 1:* (Ch 5, sc in ring) twice; ch 5, turn.

*Row 2:* Sc in ch-5 lp, ch 5, sc in next ch-5 lp; ch 5, turn.

*Row 3:* Sc in 1st ch-5 lp, ch 5, sc in same lp; ch 5, sc in next ch-5 lp, ch 5, turn. *Row 4:* Sc in 1st ch-5 lp, (ch 5, sc in next ch-5 lp) twice; ch 5, turn. *Row 5* (increase row): Sc in 1st ch-5 lp, ch 5, sc in same lp; (ch 5, sc in next ch-5 lp) twice; ch 5, turn.

*Rows 6-8:* Rep Row 4, rep bet ( )'s 3 times. *Row 9:* Rep Row 5, rep bet ( )'s 3 times. *Rows 10-12:* Rep Row 4, rep bet ( )'s 4 times. *Row 13:* Rep Row 5, rep bet ( )'s 4 times. *Rows 14-16:* Rep Row 4, rep bet ( )'s 5 times. *Row 17:* Rep Row 5, rep bet ( )'s 5 times. *Rows 18-20:* Rep Row 4, rep bet ( )'s 6 times.

*Row 21:* Rep Row 5, rep bet ( )'s 6 times. *Rows 22-24:* Rep Row 4, rep bet ( )'s 7 times. *Row 25:* Rep Row 4, rep bet ( )'s 6 times; ch 2, dc in last ch-lp, ch 5, turn.

*Row 26:* Sk ch-2 lp, sc in next ch-5 lp, (ch 5, sc in next ch-5 lp) 6 times; ch 5, turn. *Row 27:* Rep Row 4, rep bet ( )'s 5 times; ch 2, dc in last ch-lp; ch 5, turn.

*Row 28:* Sk ch-2 lp, sc in next ch-5 lp; (ch 5, sc in next ch-5 lp) 4 times; ch 2, dc in next ch-lp; ch 5, turn. *Row 29:* Rep Row 28, rep bet ( )'s 3 times. *Row 30:* Rep Row 28, rep bet ( )'s 2 times. *Row 31:* Rep Row 28, rep bet ( )'s once. *Row 32:* Dc in next ch-5 lp, ch 5, sc in next lp. Fasten off.

WING EDGING: *Rnd 1:* Working along the *inside* lower edge of wing, join thread in the ch-8 ring at bottom tip of wing; work 6 sc in same lp; work 3 sc in each turning lp until wing begins to slant. Ch 3, work 4 dc in each turning ch-lp around ending 4 dc in the ch-8 lp at beg of rnd; ch 1, join to 1st sc.

*Rnd 2:* Sc in each sc to the 1st dc, ch 1, sc in 1st dc, * hdc in next dc, 3 dc in next dc, hdc in next dc, sc in next dc, sl st in next dc, sc in next dc; rep from * around to 1st sc at tip of wing.

*Rnd 3:* Sc in each sc to beg of 1st scallop, ch 3, sc in center sc of 3-dc-grp; * ch 5, sc in center sc of next 3-dc-group. Rep from * around the scallop edge only; join to 1st sc. Fasten off.

Stiffen wing (see cornucopia ornament instructions, on page 19). When dry, add gold edging as follows: *Rnd 4:* Join gold thread in 1st ch-5 lp at each end and in same lp and in each ch-5 lp work (sc, hdc, dc, ch 2, dc, hdc, sc); fasten off.

HEAD: Beg at bottom of head, ch 2, work 5 sc in 2nd ch from hook; do not join, place marker on last st to mark beg of rnd. *Rnd 2-3:* 2 sc in each sc around—20 sc end of Rnd 3. *Rnd 4:* Sc in next sc, 2 sc in next sc—30 sc. *Rnd 5:* Sc in next 3 sc, 2 sc in next sc—50 sc. Work even for ½ inch.

*Next rnd:* * Sc in each of next 4 sc, 2 sc in next sc; rep from * around—60 sc.

Work even for 1 inch. Place egg in head and continue working in sc's around and at the same time work dec's as you work to fit the shape. Work only until the crochet is about ½ inch from top of head. Hair will cover the remaining part of the head. Fasten off.

COLLAR: With gold, ch 10; join to make ring. Ch 4, work 23 trc in ring. Fasten off. Set aside.

HALO: With gold thread, ch 4, join to make ring.

*Rnd 1:* Ch 1, work 9 sc in ring; join to 1st sc. *Rnd 2:* Ch 5, dc in next sc, * ch 2, dc in next sc, rep from * around; join to 3rd ch of beg ch-5. *Rnd 3:* Ch 3, * 2 dc in next ch-2 sp, dc in next dc, rep from * around; join to top of ch-3.

*Rnd 4:* Working in dc's, rep Rnd 2. *Rnd 5:* Ch 6, * trc in next dc, ch 2, rep from * around; join to 4th ch of beg ch-6.

*Rnd 6:* Working over ch-2 lps and 12-inch piece of wire, in each ch-2 sp around, work sc, 2 dc, sc; join to 1st sc. Fasten off. Form a circle from wire, cut to fit finish size of halo; slip through outside edge of halo.

### Stiffening and finishing

To stiffen, see instructions for cornucopia ornaments, page 19.

Place dress over a plastic foam cone after it is dipped in glue mixture. Pull sleeves out and shape as desired. Crinkle long strands of plastic wrap and place under the skirt to hold its fullness as it dries. Allow to dry thoroughly. Tack wings in place. Slip collar over neck; glue head to neck edge.

HAIR: Cut about fifty 12-inch yarn lengths. Center yarn on a 2½-inch piece of tape; sew down center. Repeat the layering. Remove tape, glue wig to head, and trim hair. Pin halo to head.

# Cameo Rose Ornaments

Shown on page 7.

Finished size is 4½x4½ inches.

### MATERIALS
DMC Cébélia cotton crochet thread, Size 30 (two 563-yard balls of white and one ball *each* of pink and green yield 12 ornaments total)
No. 10 steel hook
15 inches of ½-inch-wide white lace (for each ornament)

**Abbreviations:** See page 53.
**Gauge:** 6 spaces equal 1 inch; 5½ rows equal 1 inch.

*continued*

# CRAFT A MERRY CHRISTMAS

## INSTRUCTIONS

*Note:* The ornament may be crocheted in one solid color as with any other filet crochet pattern, following chart and having (dc, ch 2, dc) for open mesh and 2 dc in place of the ch-2 for the blocks. For ease of construction, roses are worked into a continuous strip of mesh, then stiffened and cut into desired shape.

## Hints on working cameo crochet

As each color row is worked, keep in mind where the thread will need to be in order to start the next row; often it can be taken to the proper place with a series of sl st. In a few instances the thread will need to be cut and reattached, but avoid this where possible. To attach mesh section to the side of a block, dc in last available mesh dc, then dc in top corner of colored block to make last space. After the increase of pink blocks is completed on Row 15 it will be possible to work back and forth and completely finish remainder of rose before continuing with white sections or starting leaves. Weave all ends neatly into a section of matching color.

With white, ch 128 loosely. *Row 1:* Dc in 8th ch from hook, (ch 2, sk 2 ch, dc in next ch) across for a total of 41 spaces. Ch 5, turn. *Row 2:* Dc in next dc, (ch 2, dc in next dc) across, dc in 3rd st of initial ch-5 at end of row. Ch 5, turn. Rep Row 2 until a total of 9 rows of plain mesh are made.

*Rows 10 and 11:* From now on, side of work facing when making even numbered rows will be called "front side." Continuing with white, make 17 spaces across front side, turn back and sl st across top of last 3 spaces just made, sl st in 4th dc, ch 5, dc in next dc, (ch 2, dc in next dc) 13 times for a total of 14 spaces. Drop white but do not break off.

## Starting pink rose

Turn to front side, attach pink to top left corner of 17th white mesh, ch 2, dc in next dc, (2 dc over next space, dc in next dc) twice—2 blocks made. Drop pink, attach another white thread to top left corner of 2nd pink block, ch 2, dc in next dc, work plain mesh across to end, drop white.

With pink, sl st across top of 1st 2 white spaces and in 2nd white dc, ch 3, turn. Make (2 dc in next space, dc in next dc) twice, dc in next 3 dc, ch 2, sk 2 dc, dc in next dc, (2 dc over next space, dc in next dc) 3 times, ch 2, sl st in 3rd st of white ch-5. Drop pink.

Pick up 2nd white thread, finish Row 11 by making ch 5 and turn, then work across back side in plain mesh, end with ch 2 and sl st in dc at end of pink block.

Continuing to follow chart, use pink and green blocks as shown for rose and leaves, attaching side mesh sections to ends of blocks. When colored rows are completed work 19 rows plain white mesh, then start next rose. After desired number of flowers are made work 9 rows and fasten off.

## Stiffening and finishing the ornaments

See cornucopia ornament instructions below. Stretch and pin crochet to large sheet of cardboard; allow to dry.

Remove pins. Cut crochet into heart shapes. Trim with lace; attach bows and loops for hanging.

# Cornucopia Ornaments

Shown on pages 8–9.

Finished size is 7 inches long.

## MATERIALS

DMC No. 8 white pearl cotton floss (two 95-yard balls will make three ornaments)
Size 9 steel crochet hook
Plastic cones; aluminum foil
Rustproof pins; glue
Large square of cardboard

**Abbreviations:** See page 53.

## INSTRUCTIONS

Ch 5, join with sl st to form ring. *Rnd 1:* Ch 3, make 9 dc in ring, join in top of ch-3. *Rnd 2:* Ch 3, dc in each dc around, join in top of ch-3. *Rnd 3:* Ch 3, dc in same place as joining, 2 dc in each of other 9 dc around, join in top of ch-3. *Rnd 4:* Rep Rnd 2.

*Rnd 5:* Ch 6, (sk next dc, trc in next dc, ch 2) around, join in 4th st of ch-6. *Rnd 6:* Sl st in 1st space, ch 3, make dc, ch 2, and 2 dc in same sp (starting shell made). * Ch 4, sk 1 sp, make shell of (2 dc, ch 2, 2 dc) in next space.

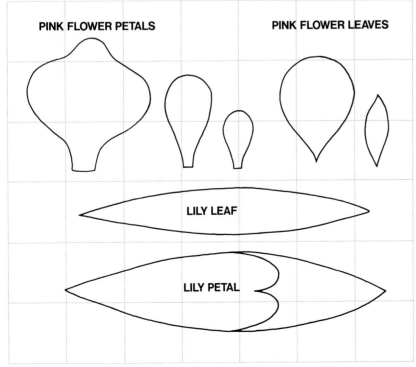

PINK FLOWER PETALS

PINK FLOWER LEAVES

LILY LEAF

LILY PETAL

1 Square = 1 Inch

Rep from * around, end with ch 4 and sl st in top of ch-3.

*Rnd 7:* Sl st to center of 1st shell, ch 3 and make starting shell in same sp. * Ch 2, sc over lp of previous row, ch 2, shell in next shell. Rep from * around, join in top of ch-3. *Rnd 8:* (Shell in shell, ch 5) all around, join as before. *Rnd 9:* (Shell in shell, ch 3, sc over lp of previous row, ch 3) all around, join.

*Rnd 10:* Ch 6, * trc in center of shell, ch 2, trc in last dc of shell, ch 2, trc in sc, ch 2, trc in 1st dc of next shell, ch 2. Rep from * around, join in 4th st of ch-6. *Rnd 11:* Sl st in 1st sp, make starting shell in same place. * Ch 2, sk 1 sp, shell in next sp. Rep from * around, join in top of ch-3. (Total of 10 shells.) *Rnd 12:* Same as Rnd 7.

*Rnd 13:* Shell in each shell around, with ch-3 bet. *Rnd 14:* Same as Rnd 7. *Rnd 15:* Shell in each shell, with ch-4 bet.

*Rnd 16:* Same as Rnd 7.

*Rnd 17:* Same as Rnd 15.

*Rnd 18:* Same as Rnd 9.

*Rnds 19 and 20:* Same as Rnds 8 and 9.

*Rnd 21:* Same as Rnd 10.

*Rnd 22:* Sc in same place as joining, (ch 6, sc in next trc) around, end with ch 3, dc in 1st sc made. *Rnd 23:* Sc in same place as joining, (ch 7, sc in next lp) around, end with ch 3, trc in 1st sc made.

*Rnds 24 and 25:* Same as Rnd 23, having ch-8 for each lp and ending with ch 4 and trc in 1st sc made. *Rnd 26:* Sc in same place as joining. * In next lp make (trc, ch 5, sl st in top of trc just made) 8 times, trc in same lp, sc in next lp. Rep from * around, join in 1st sc made. Fasten off.

**Stiffening**

Stretch cornucopia over plastic cone; mark cone at spot where ruffle *begins* with a pin. Cut cone at this point. Cover cone and cardboard with aluminum foil.

Mix glue and water together in equal parts, adding just a little more water to the solution. Dip cornucopia into solution, squeeze out excess glue, and stretch cornucopia over cone; pin along the bottom edge.

Place cone on cardboard. Then, stretch and pin ruffle to cardboard. Allow to dry, but remove before it dries thoroughly; bend one side of ruffle down. Attach ribbon loop hanger.

# Cornucopia Centerpiece

Shown on page 8.

Finished size is 16 inches long.

**MATERIALS**
DMC Cébélia crochet cotton, Size 10, two 50-gram (282-yard) balls white
No. 8 steel crochet hook
Aluminum foil; rustproof pins
Cardboard; plastic cone; glue

**Abbreviations:** See page 53.

**INSTRUCTIONS**

Ch 5, join with sl st to form ring. *Rnd 1:* Ch 3, make 9 dc in ring, join in top of ch-3. *Rnd 2:* Ch 3, dc in each dc around, join in top of ch-3. *Rnd 3:* Ch 4, (dc in next dc, ch 1) 9 times, join in 3rd st of ch-4. *Rnd 4:* Ch 5, (trc in next dc, ch 1) 9 times, join in 4th st of ch-5.

*Rnds 5 and 6:* Ch 6, (trc in next trc, ch 2) 9 times, join in 4th st of ch-6. *Rnd 7:* Ch 4, trc in same place as joining, (ch 2, 2 trc in next trc) 9 times, ch 2, join in top of ch-4. *Rnd 8:* Ch 4, trc in next trc, (ch 2, trc in each of next 2 trc) 9 times, ch 2, join in top of ch-4. *Rnd 9:* Ch 4, trc in same place as joining, trc in next trc, (ch 2, 2 trc in next trc, trc in next trc) 9 times, ch 2, join in top of ch-4. *Rnds 10-12:* Ch 4, trc in each trc around with ch-2 sp bet solid grps, join in top of ch-4. *Rnd 13:* Ch 4, trc in same place as joining, trc in next trc, 2 trc in last trc, (ch 2, 2 trc in 1st trc, trc in center trc, 2 trc in last trc) 9 times, join in top of ch-4.

*Rnds 14-17:* Ch 4, make 5 trc in each solid grp around with ch-2 sp bet each group. (Initial ch-4 counts as the 1st trc.) *Rnd 18:* Work 2 trc in 1st and last trc of each solid grp so there are 7 trc total, with ch-2 space bet each grp. *Rnds 19-22:* Make 7 trc in each grp, ch-2 bet.

*Rnds 23-27:* Increasing as before, have 9 trc in each grp, ch-2 bet. *Rnds 28-32:* Make 11 trc in each grp, ch-2 bet. *Rnds 33 and 34:* Make 13 trc in each grp, ch-2 bet. *Rnd 35:* Ch 6, * (sk 1 trc, trc in next trc, ch 2) 6 times, trc in 1st trc of next grp, ch 2. Rep from * around, join in 4th st of ch-6. *Rnd 36* (start ruffle): Sc in same place as joining, (ch 6, sc in next trc) around, end with ch 3, dc in 1st sc made. *Rnds 37-40:* Sc in center of joining lp (ch 6, sc in center of next lp) around, end with ch 3, dc in 1st sc made. *Rnds 41-44:* Sc in center of joining lp, (ch 7, sc in center of next lp) around, end with ch 3, trc in 1st sc made.

*Rnds 45-47:* Sc in center of joining lp, (ch 8, sc in center of next lp) around, end with ch 4, trc in 1st sc made. *Rnd 48:* Sc in center of joining lp, * make trc in next lp, (ch 3, sl st in top of last trc made, 3 trc in same lp) 3 times, sc in center of next lp. Rep from * around, join in 1st sc made. Fasten off.

**Stiffening**

See instructions for the cornucopia ornaments above.

# Crepe Paper Angel

Shown on page 10.

Finished size is 13 inches tall.

**MATERIALS**
Super Crepe (available at craft and hobby stores)
20-gauge wire; floral tape
Egg-shaped plastic foam ball for head
Wool roving for hair
Artificial flower centers
Cardboard for base and wings
Fabric dye; thread
Tape; cotton balls; glue; pins

*continued*

## INSTRUCTIONS

HEAD: Wrap thread around middle of 3-inch-wide piece of crepe. Place foam ball in center (thread will be at top of head); cover ball completely. Wrap thread around bottom of ball to form neck. Slide a 6-inch wire through neck and head.

ARMS: Cut an 11-inch length of wire. Bend ends inward ¾ inch to form loops (hands). Thread a ¾-inch-wide strip of crepe through each hand and wrap around the loops and to the middle of the wire, adding strips as necessary. Wrap thread around the hands and arms to secure.

SLEEVES: Gather 6-inch-wide pink crepe around each wrist, extending crepe out over the hands; wrap tightly with thread. Full the crepe back over arm, shaping a puffed sleeve; wrap near center of wire (shoulders). Push head wire through center of arms and wrap.

TORSO: Place two cotton balls side by side in center of vertically positioned crepe for bust. Fold long sides toward center; fold crepe in half widthwise. Wrap thread around bottom to form waist. Position this section on front of neck wire, ½ inch below neck. Wrap thread over shoulder and around waist to secure.

WINGS: Enlarge pattern on page 14. Trace individual units onto posterboard; cut out. Glue crepe paper to both sides of posterboard; trim. Weight wing sections when drying to prevent curling. Before wing Section D dries, fold in half.
Glue sections together to form wings. Make a tab to attach wings by cutting ¼-inch slits ¼ inch from straight edge of wing; at top and bottom, bend tab to back side of wing. Attach wings to bodice

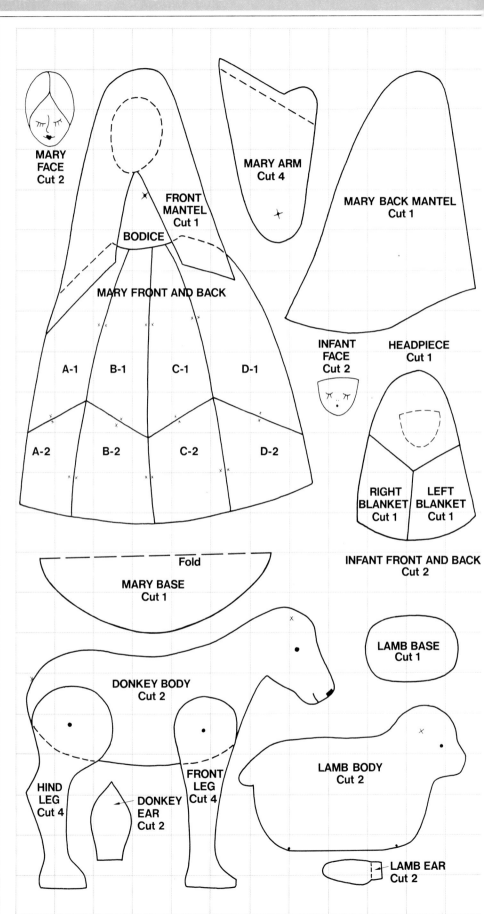

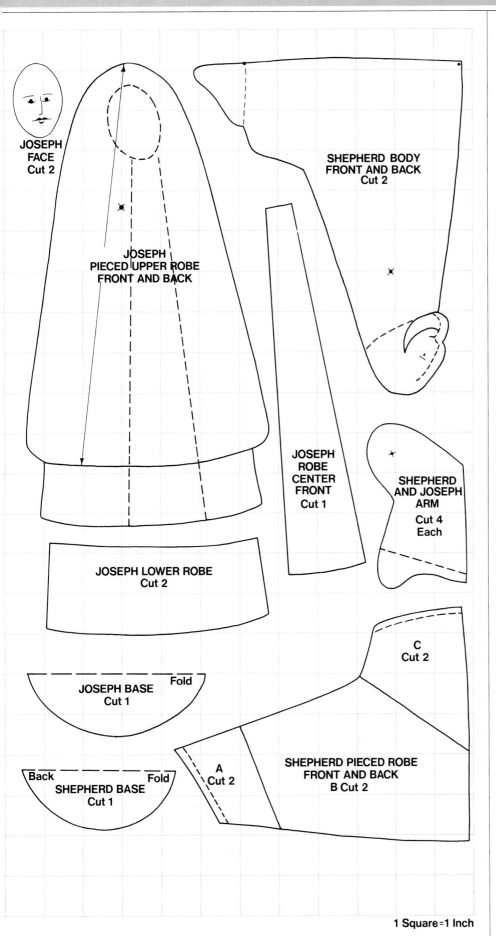

**JOSEPH FACE** Cut 2

**JOSEPH PIECED UPPER ROBE FRONT AND BACK**

**SHEPHERD BODY FRONT AND BACK** Cut 2

**JOSEPH ROBE CENTER FRONT** Cut 1

**SHEPHERD AND JOSEPH ARM** Cut 4 Each

**JOSEPH LOWER ROBE** Cut 2

**JOSEPH BASE** Cut 1 — Fold

**SHEPHERD BASE** Cut 1 — Back — Fold

**A** Cut 2

**SHEPHERD PIECED ROBE FRONT AND BACK** B Cut 2

**C** Cut 2

1 Square = 1 Inch

after first layer is completed. Position wings, wrap thread through slits and around doll, wrapping until completely secure.

BODICE: Center a 3-inch-wide strip of pink crepe on each shoulder; cross crepe over bust in front and back, gathering at waist. Secure with thread, wrapping crepe below waist tightly to wire. Repeat with two more pieces of crepe, pleating at shoulders.

SKIRT: Cut a cardboard half-circle (15-inch diameter). Bend into a cone that is approximately 5 inches in diameter across bottom; opening at top is 1 inch wide.

For bottom skirt layer, cut an 18-inch-wide piece of crepe paper. Secure to top of cone with pins and thread. Glue crepe at top; remove pins when dry. To drape skirt, stretch paper in opposite directions every ½ inch.

For top skirt, cut pink crepe to fit half of cone; scallop bottom. Repeat for back; glue at top and sides. Curl scallops around pencil. Insert bodice through opening in cone top. Secure to skirt with a long needle, pushing it through skirt, bodice, and on through to other side of skirt. Glue waist area from inside cone; remove needle when dry. Cut ½-inch strip of crepe for belt; tie around waist.

HAIR: Sew wool roving into place. Use bobby pins and hair spray to form curls. Glue flower atop hair.

FLOWERS: Secure flower centers to wire with thread. Cut spoon-shaped petals in desired sizes and wrap tips around a pencil to curl. Stretch petal centers inward.

One petal at a time, secure petal around stem by wrapping ends with thread. When petals are in place, glue thread ends.

Wrap stem with floral tape, adding leaves as desired.

To make the buds, cover a cotton ball with crepe paper, using thread to secure to wire. Add leaves; cover stem with floral tape. Attach flowers to hand.

# CRAFT A MERRY CHRISTMAS

## Crepe Paper Wreath

Shown on page 11.

**MATERIALS**
White crepe paper
Fabric dyes (green, pink, purple)
16-inch macrame hoop
1 package of baby's breath
Purple and yellow tempera paint
Paintbrushes
Purple dry marker
Floral tape
19-gauge wire
Cloth-covered wire (stamens and corkscrew shapes)
White bread
Glue
Bleach
Plastic stencil paper
Purchased black flower stamens

**INSTRUCTIONS**
Enlarge patterns, page 18, onto paper; cut out.
*Note:* Cut out two stencils from plastic stencil paper for lily petal.

### Leaves
Cut the package of crepe paper into fourths for easier handling. Follow the dye instructions and handle the crepe paper just as you would handle fabric.
Dye the crepe paper in shades of dark evergreen, olive, and celery; when the paper has reached the desired shade, place it on the rack of a low oven to dry.
Cut 20 lily leaves from celery and olive green; cut more as needed. For variety, cut leaves shorter and narrower, if desired.
Cut 20 pink flower leaves from evergreen; cut more as needed.

### Lily flower
PETALS: Cut five petals for *each* flower from white crepe paper. Place the heart-shaped stencil over the petal and paint with yellow. Lay the reverse stencil over the yellow area and paint uncovered area with purple. Add purple dots to petals with dry marker. Make enough petals for five lilies.
Repeat the process for the lily buds, cutting three petals for each bud; make enough for six lily buds.

STAMENS: Make stamens from white bread and glue. First, trim off the crusts. Use 1 tbsp. of glue for each slice of bread. Knead glue and yellow paint into the bread. Shape dough into ovals to form stamens. Push cloth-covered wire through the stamens. Let dry. Make six for *each* lily flower.

ASSEMBLY: Wrap floral tape around six stamens and onto a 7-inch wire. Wrap petals and leaves onto wire to form lily. Repeat for buds, eliminating stamens.

### Pink flowers
Dye the crepe pink and evergreen as directed for leaves. Cut one large and two medium petals from pink and one small petal from white (flower center). Cut enough for 13 flowers. Cut out leaves.
Stretch the small and medium petals to form a cupped shape.
Wrap cloth covered wire around a pencil to form spring shape.
Secure the petals, leaves, and spring shaped wire onto 19-gauge wire using floral tape.

### Vine flowers
Dye the crepe paper purple and use leftover pink crepe paper (from pink flowers) to make the vine flowers; use the pattern for the smallest pink flower petal for vine flower pattern. Cut 16 petals for *each* vine flower; make enough for 13 vines.
Wrap floral tape around the 19-gauge wire, inserting black flower stamens at the top.
Place glue on the tip of the flower petals; press and twist two petals onto wire every inch.
When the glue is dry, dip the paintbrush into bleach; put a drop on the bottom edge of each petal, letting bleach bleed into circular edge of petal; allow to dry.

### Assembling the wreath
Wrap the flowers onto a 16-inch-diameter macrame hoop using floral tape. Wrap the baby's breath onto hoop, filling in the spaces between flowers. Attach wire hanger.

## Patchwork Nativity

Shown on pages 12–13.

**MATERIALS**
¾ yard of muslin
Fabric scraps (see instructions)
Tapestry wool (brown, light brown, and black)
Embroidery floss in desired colors
Scraps of lace and ribbon (Mary and Infant)
Gray and brown felt scraps
Polyester fiberfill
Twigs for staff and cradle
Glue; powdered rouge
Gold cardboard and trim for halo
Black beads for animal eyes

**INSTRUCTIONS**
Enlarge patterns, pages 20–21, onto paper. A ¼-inch seam is included, unless otherwise stated.
For each figure, cut the outline from muslin—one front and one back. All other fabric pieces are patched onto muslin fronts and backs. Cut arms from muslin.

### Mary
Cut out paper patterns. Make separate patterns for the eight skirt sections. Add ⅛-inch seams to all inside edges of skirt sections (indicated by Xs on pattern).

FRONT: Cut bodice from beige fabric, slightly larger than the area it covers. Baste in place.
Cut skirt sections from four prints. Seam two parts of each skirt section (A-1 and A-2) together using ⅛-inch seams; baste section A to muslin front.
With right sides facing and using ⅛-inch seams, sew section B to A, sewing through muslin. Fold B to front; press. Sew section C to B in same manner. Repeat for section D. Baste bottom edge of skirt to muslin. Trim waist with ribbon. Work featherstitches on skirt.

MANTLE: Cut the mantle from blue fabric. Stay-stitch ⅛ inch from inside curve. Place atop muslin; baste outside edges. Turn under inside edges; blindstitch.

FACE: Transfer pattern to muslin. Embroider features using a single floss strand. Stay-stitch around face outline. Cut out ¼ inch from stitching; appliqué.

HAIR: Using one strand of light brown tapestry wool, embroider straight stitches for hair. Work French knots at side of face. Color cheeks with rouge. Frame hair with lace.

ARMS: Use arm pattern for sleeve pattern, eliminating hand portion. Cut four sleeves from a fifth print fabric. For each arm, turn under straight edge ¼ inch; topstitch to muslin arm along dashed line. Baste sleeve to arm.

Sew one arm together, right sides facing, leaving an opening. Clip curves, turn, stuff, and sew opening. Repeat for other arm.

BACK: Patch back in the same manner as directed above, reversing direction on skirt pieces. Exclude bodice section and use the pattern for back mantle. Baste mantle in place, turn under bottom edge and sew to skirt.

ASSEMBLY: Sew front to back, right sides facing, leaving bottom edge open. Use ¼-inch seams. Clip curves and turn. Baste under ¼ inch on bottom edge; stuff.

Draw base pattern onto blue fabric. Sew on this line; cut base ¼ inch from stay stitching. Baste under raw edge. Sew base to bottom of figure; remove basting.

Attach arms to body.

HALO: Cut a 3¼-inch-diameter circle from gold cardboard. Glue gold trim around outside edge. Glue to back of head.

### Infant

Piece muslin front as indicated on pattern using three blue print fabrics. Trim bottom of headpiece with ribbon. Embroider over the seams of the patchwork.

Follow instructions for Mary's face to sew Infant's face. Trim head with lace.

Cut back from blue print; baste to muslin back. Join front and back, right sides facing, leaving

opening at bottom. Clip curves, turn, stuff, and sew opening.

Cut a 2¼-inch-diameter gold circle (halo); finish as for Mary.

### Joseph

FRONT AND BACK: Piece 1½-inch squares to make a rectangle with 10 rows of six squares *each*.

Cut the upper robe front from pieced fabric. Baste outside edges to muslin front. Using black thread, quilt an X in every other square. Cut the upper robe back from solid fabric. Baste in place.

Cut bottom robe piece from dark blue print; sew top edge of this piece to bottom edge of top robe. Baste remaining edges to muslin; repeat for back.

Cut out center front panel from solid blue fabric; press under ¼ inch on each side. Blindstitch to dashed lines of pattern.

FACE: Follow instructions for Mary's face. Straight-stitch beard using black tapestry wool.

ASSEMBLY AND ARMS: Work as directed for Mary.

HEAD PIECE: Cut a 6½x13-inch blue print rectangle. Tack in place; tie cord around head.

Glue twig staff to hand.

### Shepherd

FRONT AND BACK: Piece front and back muslin pieces using burlap and pumpkin-color fabric. Turn under top edge of pieced front and back to form neckline; topstitch. Turn under raw edge of pieced front and back to form bottom edge of robe (dashed lines on pattern).

With right sides facing, join front and back, beginning and ending at dots.

Finish assembling figure as described for Mary. Work blanket stitches over seams of patched fabric with brown tapestry wool.

FACE: Embroider features. Use brown tapestry wool and straight stitches to stitch beard.

HEAD PIECE: Cut a 10-inch square of burlap in half diagonally. Using one of the triangles, fold

under raw edge on longest side; wrap this edge over head; tack folds of fabric in place. Tie yarn around head to secure head piece.

### Cradle

Cut nine 5-inch-long twigs. Cross two twigs to form an X; tie together at intersection. Repeat with two more twigs (these are the ends of the cradle). Connect the ends with a third twig by gluing the ends of the third twig across the intersection of each end. Glue two twigs up each side. Fill with excelsior or straw.

### For lamb

On *double thickness* of white nubby fabric, draw around lamb pattern. *Do not add seam allowances.* Sew on the drawn line, leaving bottom edge open.

Trim away excess fabric, clip curves, turn, and stuff.

Baste under raw edge. Attach base as directed for Mary.

Cut ears from gray felt. Fold over flap; sew ears to head.

Sew black bead eyes in place.

### Donkey

BODY: Piece two 6x8-inch rectangles using beige, dark brown, and brown checked wool fabrics.

On wrong side of one rectangle, draw around the body pattern. With right sides of pieced rectangles facing, sew along *drawn* line, leaving bottom open. Trim excess fabric, clip curves, and turn. Stuff and sew opening closed.

HEAD: Sew bead eyes in place. With brown floss, outline-stitch a grin; satin-stitch the nose.

Use tapestry wool and Rya knots for mane. Clip loops. Make tassel at end of a length of wool for tail; tack in place.

Cut two ears from brown felt. Fold bottom edges together to cup the ears; stitch to head at X.

LEGS: On a *double thickness of fabric* draw around leg pattern. Sew on this drawn line, leaving an opening for turning. Trim excess fabric, clip curves, turn, and stuff; sew opening. Make two from checked wool, and two from beige. Attach legs at dots to body.

# NEEDLEPOINT POINSETTIA WREATH

Subtle shading and realistic detail turn this elegant white poinsettia wreath, *left*, into a stitchery masterpiece.

Make the most of this lovely design by stitching gifts using the same motifs. For example, you might craft a box, *below*, or the ornaments and gift tags pictured on the following pages.

# Needlepoint Poinsettia Wreath

Finished size, framed, is about 27x27 inches.

## MATERIALS
30-inch square of 14-count needlepoint canvas
3-ply Persian needlepoint yarn in peach and the colors listed in the color key, page 29
Needlepoint frame or artist's stretcher strips
Tapestry needle
Water-soluble marking pen
Masking tape

## INSTRUCTIONS

### Beginning the piece
Bind the edges of the needlepoint canvas with masking tape to prevent raveling.

Using a yardstick, measure both horizontally and vertically to determine the *exact* center of the canvas piece. Mark this point with a water-soluble marker.

From this point, count upward 60 stitches; mark this point. This represents the beginning stitch of the design, which is indicated by an arrow on the pattern, page 29.

Mount the canvas on stretcher strips or a frame to avoid distortion and to make blocking easier.

### Stitching the piece
The wreath pattern, pages 28–29, is a repeat design and makes up one quarter of the total wreath.

To complete the wreath, shift the quadrant three times to complete the circle. Follow the pattern to complete the first quadrant. Begin the other quadrants by stitching from the end of each of the previous sections.

Work the motifs in continental stitches using two plies of yarn.

When the flowers are complete, work "Joy," page 29, in the center of the wreath.

Fill in the background color using basketweave stitches.

### Finishing
*To block* the piece, dampen the canvas and, with rustproof T-pins, mount it on a blocking board. Sprinkle with water; allow the canvas to dry thoroughly before removing it from the board.

*To frame* the needlepoint, mount the canvas on a plywood board the same size as the finished needlework. (Pad the board with one or more layers of quilt batting.) Stretch the needlepoint over the board, keeping the corners square; staple it securely to the back.

Or, mount the canvas on artist's stretcher strips cut to size, assembled, and stabilized with angle irons.

Cut and assemble the picture molding of your choice for a frame, or take the board to a local framer for professional finishing.

# Cross-Stitched Heart Box

Finished size of insert is 10x10 inches.

## MATERIALS
13x13 inches of white hardanger
Embroidery floss (see color key)
Embroidery hoop
Tapestry needle
Heart-shape box (available at craft shops or write to: Plain n' Fancy, Inc., P.O. Box 756, Jensen Beach, FL 33457)
Polyester batting
Graph paper
Felt-tip markers
Staple gun
Masking tape
Water-soluble marking pen

## INSTRUCTIONS

### Preparing the pattern
Use the single poinsettia motif, pages 28–29, for the box design.

Chart the pattern onto graph paper using felt-tip markers.

### Preparing the materials

Tape raw edges of the fabric to prevent threads from raveling.

Determine the center of the pattern and the center of the fabric; mark these center points with a water-soluble pen. (Begin cross-stitching here.)

Separate the embroidery floss and use two strands for stitching.

### Stitching the piece

Work cross-stitches over two threads of the fabric.

When all stitching is complete, block the piece by pressing it carefully with a damp press cloth and a warm iron.

### Finishing

Remove the heart-shape insert on the lid. Center the design atop the insert, with a layer of batting in between. Fold the excess fabric to the back side of the lid, clipping the fabric as necessary. Tape and then staple the fabric in place. Reassemble the lid.

## Needlepoint Poinsettia Ornament

Finished size is 4½ inches in diameter.

### MATERIALS
23-mesh silk needlepoint canvas
DMC embroidery floss (see color key, page 29)
Embroidery hoop
Tapestry needle
6x12-inch piece of peach fabric
Polyester fiberfill
½ yard of ⅛-inch-diameter gold metallic cording
Monofilament thread

### INSTRUCTIONS

Prepare the pattern as directed for the heart-shape box.

Determine the center of the pattern and the center of the canvas; begin stitching here.

Separate the floss and use three strands for stitching.

Work the stitchery using continental stitches. Do not fill in the background area.

When the stitchery is complete, block it following the instructions for the poinsettia wreath picture.

Draw a 4½-inch-diameter circle around the outside of the design. Cut out shape, adding a ½-inch seam allowance.

Cut out two identical shapes from peach fabric. (One is the lining for the stitchery, the other for the ornament back).

Baste the stitchery to the peach lining. Sew gold cording in place.

With right sides facing, sew the stitchery to the peach back, leaving an opening for turning.

Clip the curves, turn, and press. Stuff ornament with polyester fiberfill and then slip-stitch the opening closed. Hang ornament using monofilament thread.

## Cross-Stitched "Joy" Gift Tags

Finished size is 3½x6 inches.

### MATERIALS
Sheets of ecru perforated paper
DMC embroidery floss in color(s) of your choice
Tapestry needle
DMC metallic gold floss
Graph paper; felt-tip markers
Monofilament thread

### INSTRUCTIONS

Chart "Joy" diagram, page 29, onto graph paper using markers.

Work each cross-stitch over one square of the perforated paper.

Using double strands of metallic floss, cross-stitch the outline (represented by diagonal lines on the chart).

Use the color of your choice to fill in the design (horizontal lines on chart). Separate the embroidery floss and use two strands for working these cross-stitches.

Cut out gift tag (at least one paper space from edge of embroidery). Thread with monofilament.

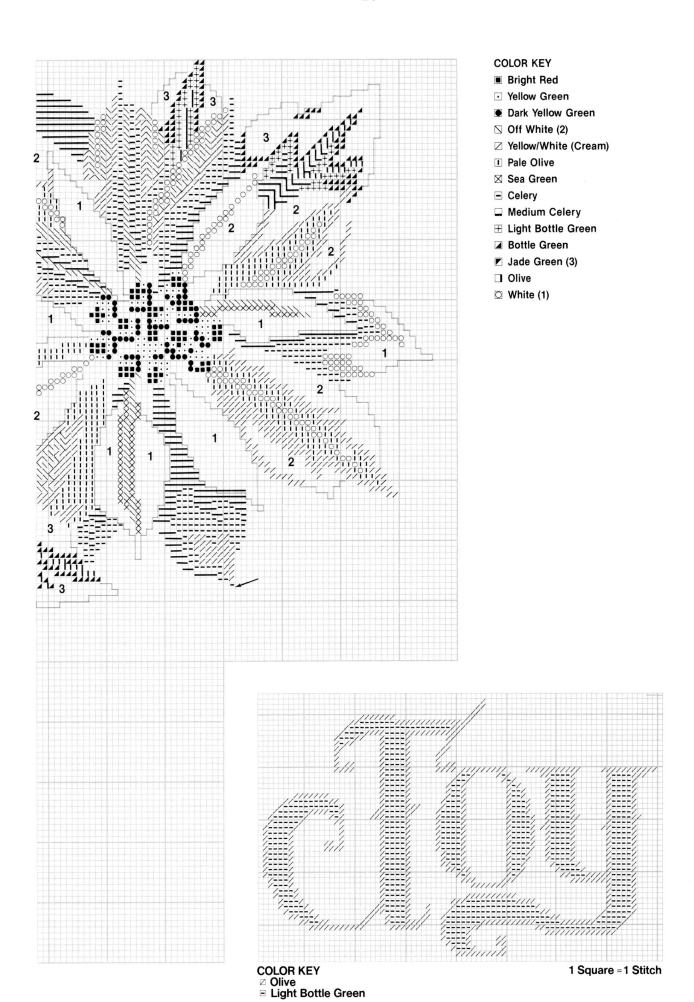

**COLOR KEY**
- ▣ Bright Red
- ⊡ Yellow Green
- ● Dark Yellow Green
- ◩ Off White (2)
- ◪ Yellow/White (Cream)
- ⊡ Pale Olive
- ⊠ Sea Green
- ⊟ Celery
- ▭ Medium Celery
- ⊞ Light Bottle Green
- ◪ Bottle Green
- ◪ Jade Green (3)
- ⬚ Olive
- ◎ White (1)

**COLOR KEY**
- ⊘ Olive
- ⊟ Light Bottle Green

**1 Square = 1 Stitch**

*Celebrate
with
Red and Green*

Holly-berry reds and evergreen greens lend warmth and familiarity to holiday festivities. These time-honored colors—symbols of the season—quickly set a holiday mood and call out "Merry Christmas" to one and all.

On the next several pages are ornaments, gifts, and accessories that will fill your home with a bold display of Christmas color.

You'll find red and green patchwork for holiday tables, a wintry landscape to cut from wood, appliqué accents, and a cheery doll in red and green garb.

The delightful smocked ornaments and wreath shown here blend the tradition of the old-world craft of smocking with Christmastime red and green. For a closer look, please turn the page. Instructions for these projects begin on page 40.

Originating in England and traveling through all of Europe, smocking is an old-world craft of pleating and decorating plain fabric that is enjoying new popularity.

The charming ornaments shown *at right* combine the old-fashioned art of smocking with holiday colors and a festive plaid fabric.

Smocking encircles a fabric covered ball, and a delicate panel accents the pretty heart. The miniature stocking is bordered with eyelet edging wide enough to allow a smocked design.

Stitch up just one or two as special trims for your tree, or make a whole treeful for your Christmas celebration.

Mother and daughter pinafores, *opposite,* are the perfect party wear for a red and green Christmas celebration. Each pinafore features an inset of smocked designs at the yoke. And red and green plaid taffeta makes them especially festive.

Stitch the pinafores using commercial patterns, adding the smocked design in place of the bib.

To make the panels, flat eyelet is gathered and stitched in a sampling of smocked patterns. Work the smocked designs on grids, transferred to the fabric in the form of evenly spaced dots.

There are two basic types of smocking: regular and English. In regular smocking, smocking stitches are worked from dot to dot, gathering the fabric in each stitch. In English smocking, running stitches are worked from dot to dot to gather the fabric; smocking stitches are then taken at each pleat or gathered in decorative designs.

Decorative variations on smocking designs are almost endless. Most of the projects shown here and on pages 30–31 are based on three basic patterns. These patterns combine the most commonly used stitches—cable, trellis, outline, and diamond.

Patterns are included for the heart, stocking, and ball ornaments, the wreath, and the child's pinafore. Follow the patterns provided, or use these stitches in different combinations to make an original design of your own.

Quick and easy decorating ideas, like those shown *opposite,* are always in demand.

The contemporary patchwork stocking is easily pieced using bold geometric shapes cut from red and green prints. The festive wreath is fashioned from lacquered napkin rings arranged in a circle. Squares of bright fabrics, tucked into each ring, masquerade as foliage.

For last-minute Christmas tree trims, craft the so-simple "hobo" ornaments. To make them, simply wrap fabric squares around plastic foam balls and secure with contrasting ribbon.

What says Christmas better than ornaments to hang and stockings to fill? Here, examples of patchwork take on a festive air with red and green fabric patches.

The design of the stocking, *above,* was inspired by antique Victorian crazy quilts, where small fabric scraps were pieced and embroidered with a sampler of stitches.

For the embroidered motifs, cut designs from inexpensive holiday handkerchiefs, or make up your own to embroider by hand.

The ornaments, *right* and *above,* are stitched in log-cabin fashion, then trimmed with embroidery, lace, and a ribbon loop.

# CELEBRATE WITH RED AND GREEN

Cheery Christmas motifs and traditional patchwork designs, worked in seasonal reds and greens, make wonderful gifts and decorations for your home.

The festive guest towels, *left*, will add a holiday touch. Stitch some to brighten your bath and give as gifts to family and friends.

Scraps of ginghams, pindots, stripes, and calicoes are machine-appliquéd on ordinary hand towels to make candy cane, candle, or Santa motifs.

Stylized Christmas trees in log cabin-fashion patchwork adorn the holiday place mats, *right*.

This simple tree design is a variation on the traditional quilt pattern. Sew an assortment of green prints into fabric yardage, cut the pieced fabric into strips, then sew the strips to a backing, and quilt. Coordinating bias strips trim the edges.

The patchwork table runner, *above,* is a welcome addition to the holiday table of any country-decor enthusiast. Make it for yourself to complement your own Christmas, or surprise a friend who loves the country look.

The runner is a sampler of familiar quilt patterns worked in prints and solids of red, green, and white cottons. Use the Log Cabin Four Patch, Variable Star, Pennsylvania Dutch Bird, Bear's Paw, and Water Wheel designs as shown here, or create the runner using your own favorite motifs.

Piece each square individually, then assemble and quilt the runner by hand or machine.

A prairie point edging in various red prints adds a finishing touch.

# CELEBRATE WITH RED AND GREEN

For holiday get-togethers this Christmas, why not stitch up a festive cloth that has just a touch of country? Bold contemporary fabrics with a hint of country charm border a central square for the quick-to-make holiday tablecloth shown *above*.

Stitch a sampling of border rectangles and corner squares around the center square and bind the outside edges with bias tape. (This tablecloth is so easy to stitch, you can make several in an evening for last-minute gift-giving occasions.)

The cloth measures 60 inches square, but you can easily alter the size to fit your table or that of a friend.

A serene winter landscape with snow-covered hills, evergreens, and bright red barns, *right,* is a perfect gift for country-loving folk.

Construct the scene from white pine lath strips. Cut each piece carefully to size and stain with a wash of acrylic paint before assembling the scene.

The just-right-for-Christmas winter scene will be a refreshing reminder of holiday warmth and friendship all year long.

Enchant doll lovers, young and old alike, with this endearing ragamuffin, *left.*

Scraps of muslin, lace, and a homespun dishtowel (stitched into a festive pinafore) make her cute, cuddly, and decidedly country.

Fashion her hair style using nubby, novelty yarn. Facial features are embroidered with strands of floss.

Her pert straw hat and miniature basket are store-bought accessories.

For instructions to craft the projects shown here, turn the page.

## Smocked Ball Ornaments

Shown on pages 30–32.

### MATERIALS

*(For one ball)*
8x32 inches of white fabric
Red, green, and white
  embroidery floss
1 yard of ¼-inch-wide satin
  ribbon (for ball top)
2½- or 3-inch plastic foam ball
Filigree cap; hanger
Straight pins

### INSTRUCTIONS

#### General instructions

The projects below use the English method of smocking. (Fabric is pleated on the *wrong* side *before* the smocking stitches are worked on the *right* side.) For pleating and stitch instructions, refer to books on the technique.

To pleat fabric before smocking, use iron-on dots (available in needlecraft stores) for marking the pleats, following manufacturer's instructions. Use a smock gathering machine if one is available. Or, use local or mail order pleating services provided by needlecraft and fabric stores.

#### For the ornament

Pleat white fabric with 14 basting rows, using *matching* thread for top and bottom two rows. Use *contrasting* thread for the middle

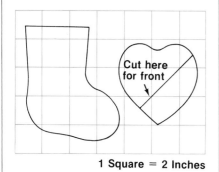

1 Square = 2 Inches

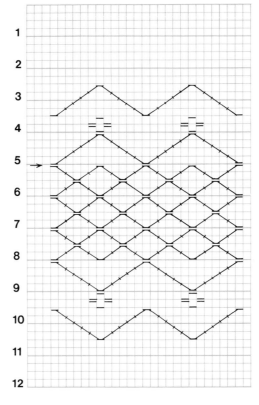

CHART A

A FULL SPACE TRELLIS

B DOUBLE FLOWERETTE

A FULL SPACE TRELLIS

B HALF SPACE TRELLIS
B HALF SPACE TRELLIS
B HALF SPACE TRELLIS
B HALF SPACE TRELLIS
B HALF SPACE TRELLIS
B HALF SPACE TRELLIS

A FULL SPACE TRELLIS

B DOUBLE FLOWERETTE

A FULL SPACE TRELLIS

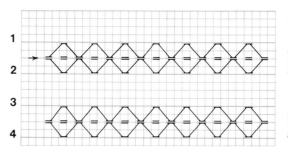

CHART B

A BABY WAVE
B SEED STITCH
A BABY WAVE

A BABY WAVE
B SEED STITCH
A BABY WAVE

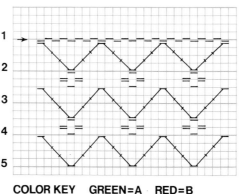

CHART C

A CABLE
A FULL SPACE TRELLIS

B DOUBLE FLOWERETTE

A FULL SPACE TRELLIS

B DOUBLE FLOWERETTE

A FULL SPACE TRELLIS

COLOR KEY    GREEN=A    RED=B

rows. Gather and tie up pleats into a 6-inch width.

Smock middle 12 rows, following chart A, *opposite*, and using three strands of floss. Design is worked over 132 pleats. Backstitch rows 1, 2, 11, and 12 with parallel rows of cable stitches using white floss. Begin smocking at arrow. For a continuous pattern on the finished ball, work design only in *complete* repeats (avoid stitching half of a repeat).

When smocking is complete, untie *matching* threads and remove *contrasting* threads. Match design lines and slip-stitch fabric together to form a tube. Slip foam ball inside tube.

Trim fabric at top and bottom so edges meet at centers. Pull *matching* threads tightly and tie; hide thread ends. Fasten fabric at the top and bottom with straight pins. Cover the bottom raw edges with filigree cap bent to fit. Add bow. Insert filigree hanger.

## Smocked Stocking Ornament

Shown on pages 30–32.

**MATERIALS**
14 inches of 3-inch-wide flat eyelet
Red and green embroidery floss
Plaid taffeta and lining fabrics
8 inches of piping
¼-inch-wide red satin ribbon (hanging loop)
Polyester fiberfill; paper

**INSTRUCTIONS**
Enlarge stocking pattern, *opposite left*, onto paper; cut out. Cut two patterns *each* from taffeta and lining fabrics.

Pleat eyelet with five basting rows, starting 1½ inches from top edge; gather to 4 inches wide and tie off basting threads. Smock the design, following chart C, *opposite*, and using three strands of floss. Design is worked over 56 pleats. Begin smocking at arrow.

Remove all but the top basting thread. Untie that thread and use

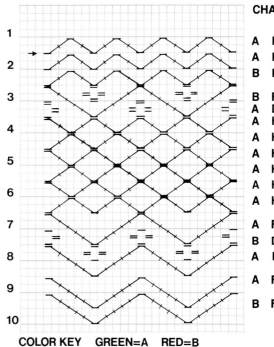

CHART D

A   HALF SPACE TRELLIS
A   HALF SPACE TRELLIS
B   HALF SPACE TRELLIS

B   FULL SPACE TRELLIS
A   DOUBLE FLOWERETTE
A   HALF SPACE TRELLIS

A   HALF SPACE TRELLIS

A   HALF SPACE TRELLIS
A   HALF SPACE TRELLIS

A   HALF SPACE TRELLIS
A   HALF SPACE TRELLIS

A   FULL SPACE TRELLIS
B   DOUBLE FLOWERETTE
A   FULL SPACE TRELLIS

A   FULL SPACE TRELLIS

B   FULL SPACE TRELLIS

COLOR KEY   GREEN=A   RED=B

it as a guide when sewing. Block smocked cuff to 4½ inches wide. Using ¼-inch seams, sew wrong side of smocked cuff to right side of stocking front along the side seams. Use ¼-inch seams to sew stocking front to back, right sides facing; leave top open. Cover piping with taffeta; sew to top edge. Sew lining, leaving a 3-inch opening at bottom. Slip right side of lining over right side of stocking. Sew around top edges. Turn and sew the lining opening closed. To hang, attach ribbon loop.

## Smocked Heart Ornament

Shown on pages 30–32.

**MATERIALS**
4x18 inches of white fabric
Plaid taffeta and lining fabrics
Red and green embroidery floss
¾ yard of 1-inch-wide pregathered eyelet
Scraps of ¼-inch-wide red satin ribbon
Polyester fiberfill
Paper

**INSTRUCTIONS**
Enlarge pattern for heart, *opposite left*, onto paper (pattern includes ¼-inch seams); cut out. Cut two from taffeta and one from lining.

Pleat fabric strip with six basting rows; gather to 3 inches wide and tie off threads. Using three strands of floss, smock four center rows, following chart B, *opposite*. Design is worked over 72 pleats. Begin smocking at arrow.

Remove basting threads from four center rows. Untie thread for rows 1 and 6. Use these threads to guide, gather, and align when stitching heart. Block smocking, stretching to length of heart inset.

Cut taffeta heart front along line indicated on pattern. Using ½-inch seams, sew inset between front pieces; sew lining to wrong side of heart. (Smocking stretches without a lining.) Sew eyelet ¼ inch from raw edges.

With right sides facing, stitch back to front leaving an opening. Turn, stuff, and stitch the opening closed. Make a ribbon hanger.

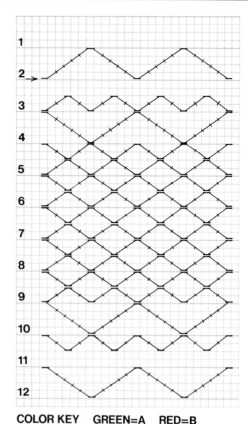

**CHART E**

A  FULL SPACE TRELLIS

B  HALF SPACE TRELLIS

B  FULL SPACE TRELLIS

B  HALF SPACE TRELLIS
A  HALF SPACE TRELLIS
A  HALF SPACE TRELLIS
A  HALF SPACE TRELLIS
A  HALF SPACE TRELLIS
A  HALF SPACE TRELLIS
A  HALF SPACE TRELLIS
A  HALF SPACE TRELLIS
A  HALF SPACE TRELLIS
B  HALF SPACE TRELLIS

B  FULL SPACE TRELLIS

B  HALF SPACE TRELLIS

A  FULL SPACE TRELLIS

COLOR KEY    GREEN=A    RED=B

## Smocked Wreath

Shown on page 31.

**MATERIALS**
10½-inch-diameter plastic foam
   wreath
6x105-inch strip of white fabric
1½ yards of plaid taffeta
Red and green embroidery floss
1 yard of 1-inch-wide
   pregathered eyelet trim
1½ yards of ⅜-inch-wide red
   satin ribbon

**INSTRUCTIONS**
Pleat fabric strip with 14 basting rows. Gather to a 21-inch
width; tie off threads. Using three
floss strands, smock 12 middle
rows. Use chart E, *above*, making
outside wreath edge a wave stitch;
work over 420 pleats. Begin
smocking at arrow.
   Untie the basting threads from
the top and bottom two rows. Remove the remaining threads.
   Seam ends to form a circle,
matching the design. Place the
smocking over the foam wreath;

draw up pleating threads to fit
around wreath. Tie threads. Remove fabric from wreath. Sew
eyelet trim to outside edge of the
smocking, keeping fullness even.
   Cut a 4x77-inch bias strip of
taffeta. Fold in half (with wrong
sides facing) lengthwise; press
and gather along raw edges to fit
outside edge of wreath. With right
sides facing, stitch taffeta ruffle
over eyelet using ½-inch seams.
   To cover back of wreath, draw
around wreath on white fabric;
cut out, *adding ½-inch seams.*
With right sides facing, join inside circle of backing fabric to the
inside circle of smocking wreath
front. Pin to wreath and stitch
outside edge, pulling fabric snug.
   Cut a 6x36-inch bias strip of
taffeta for the bow. Fold in half
lengthwise, with right sides facing. Sew together using ½-inch
seams, leaving an opening for
turning. Turn, press, and sew
closed. Tie; tack to wreath.

## Smocked Pinafores

Shown on pages 31 and 33.

**MATERIALS**
**For both pinafores**
Commercial pinafore pattern
Flat eyelet equal to height and
   three times wider than bib
   inset (not including seams)
Red, green, and white floss
Plaid taffeta fabric

**INSTRUCTIONS**

**Smocking the child's pinafore**
   Pleat 11 basting rows on the
eyelet, beginning first row 2 inches from top edge. (The 11th row
remains unsmocked for ease in
assembling pinafore.) Gather to
desired width. Using three floss
strands, smock design following
chart D, page 41. Design is
worked over 104 pleats. Smock
row 1 with white cable stitches.
Begin work at arrow. Block the
smocking to fit pattern. Sew ac-
cording to pattern instructions.

**Smocking the adult's pinafore**
   Pleat 24 basting rows in the
eyelet beginning the first row 2½
inches from top edge. (The 24th
row remains unsmocked for ease
in assembling pinafore.) Gather
to desired width. Using three floss
strands, begin by back-smocking
the first basting row with cable
stitches using white floss. Smock
pinafore, combining patterns on
pages 40–41 and *left,* as desired.
Turn work to right side. Block
smocking to size. Finish accord-
ing to pattern instructions.

## Quick-as-a-Wink Wreath, Ornaments, and Stocking

Shown on page 35.

**MATERIALS**
**For all projects**
1 yard *each* of red and green
   solid fabrics, and one white
   and three red prints
Assorted ribbons; thread

### For wreath

1⅓ yards of 72-inch-wide green Phun Phelt
14½-inch-diameter cardboard circle
Twenty-two 1¼-inch-wide wooden napkin rings
White latex paint
Fabric glue; florist's wire

### For ornaments

2½-inch-diameter foam balls
Straight pins

## INSTRUCTIONS

### For the wreath

Cut 11½-inch-diameter center from cardboard circle, leaving a 1½-inch-wide base. Wrap base with fabric strips; glue ends.

Paint the napkin rings white. When paint is dry, glue ribbon around each ring's center. Arrange rings around the base, side edges touching; wire in place.

Cut and hem 12-inch fabric squares: five from each yard of red fabrics (20 total) and 24 from green Phun Phelt. Pinch each of the squares at the center, fold loosely; slip two into each ring.

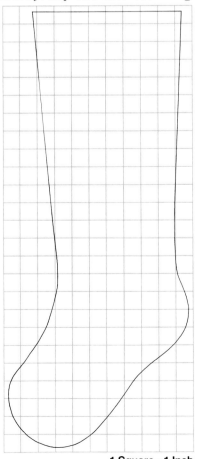

**1 Square = 1 Inch**

Use wire loop for hanging. Trim with bow.

### For the ornaments

Pin hanging loops of ¼-inch-wide ribbon at tops of foam balls. From red, white, and green fabrics cut 10-inch squares; wrap fabric around balls, gather, and tie at top with ribbon. Trim fabric.

### For the stocking

Enlarge pattern, *right.* Cut the front and back from red printed fabric. Cut patches from remaining scraps of wreath and ornament fabrics as follow: R, red; G, green; and W, white. Stitch to stocking front; cover raw edges with ribbon. Using ¼-inch seams, sew front to back, with right sides facing, leaving top open. Turn. Hem top; add bows.

# Patchwork Stocking and Ornament

Shown on page 34.

## MATERIALS

Several white handkerchiefs with embroidered Christmas designs
1 yard of red pindot fabric
⅛ yard *each* of green pindot, red, and green fabrics
39 inches of 4¼-inch-wide white pregathered eyelet
1⅔ yards *each* of ⅝-inch-wide red satin ribbon and ⅞-inch-wide red grosgrain ribbon
Embroidery floss in desired colors
2¼ yards of red piping
16x26 inches *each* of quilt batting and fleece

## INSTRUCTIONS

*Note:* Use ¼-inch seams unless otherwise indicated.

Enlarge pattern, *left,* onto paper. Add ¼-inch seams; cut out.

*For the stocking front,* cut one stocking from batting. Cut fabrics into a variety of shaped pieces. Cut embroidered designs from handkerchiefs into small shapes.

Arrange pieces on batting, alternating colors and evenly distributing handkerchief pieces.

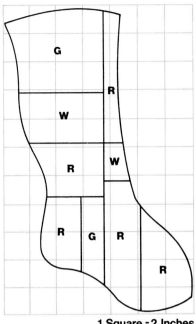

**1 Square = 2 Inches**

(Overlap some pieces and turn under ¼ inch at raw edges as needed.) Baste pieces in place.

Embroider around the pieces, using a variety of decorative stitches and beginning embroidery 4 inches from stocking top.

*For the stocking back,* cut one stocking from red pindot fabric and one from fleece. Stitch fleece to wrong side of stocking back.

Cut two stocking linings from red pindot fabric. Using ½-inch seams, sew together, right sides facing, leaving top edge open.

### Assembling the stocking

Sew piping to outer edge of stocking front. Sew front to back, right sides facing, leaving the top open. Clip curves. Turn; press.

*For the cuff,* cut eyelet in half. With right sides facing, sew short edges on one piece of eyelet together *using a 1-inch seam.* Repeat for other eyelet piece.

Sew bound edge of one eyelet piece to right side of stocking 2½ inches from top (with seam at center back). Sew bound edge of other eyelet piece to stocking top.

Sew piping to top of stocking. Press raw edge of piping to inside of stocking. Insert lining into stocking. Turn under seam on lining; sew to the piping. Attach loop for hanging. Trim with bow.

*continued*

### For the ornaments

Add ¼-inch seams to measurements. For a 4x4-inch ornament, cut a 1½-inch square for the center. Add ¾-inch-wide strips to the center in log-cabin fashion.

Trim with ½-inch-wide eyelet. Sew back to pieced front, leaving an opening. Turn, stuff, and sew opening. Attach ribbon hanger.

## Guest Towels

Shown on page 36.

Finished size is 11x18 inches.

### MATERIALS

11x18-inch guest towels
Small pieces of red, white, green, flesh, and black fabrics; red and green print fabrics
Fusible webbing
½-inch-wide red ribbon
½-inch-diameter white pom-pom

### INSTRUCTIONS

Preshrink towels and fabrics. Enlarge the patterns, *below,* and cut each pattern piece from brown paper. Referring to the photograph on page 36, cut out fabric pattern pieces. Cut a piece of fusible webbing to match each fabric piece.

Pin pieces to towel for each design as follows: *for the candle—* candle, holly leaves, flame A, flame B, and flame C; *for the stocking—* candy cane, two holly leaves in stocking, stocking, cuff, holly leaf on cuff, heel, and toe; *for Santa—* face, eyes, beard, hat, hat band, holly leaves, mustache, and nose.

*Note: For stocking,* the cuff overlaps stocking top ¼ inch. *For Santa,* the hat band overlaps hat bottom and the top of face ¼ inch; mustache overlaps bottom of face and top of beard ¼ inch.

Following the manufacturer's directions, fuse pieces in place.

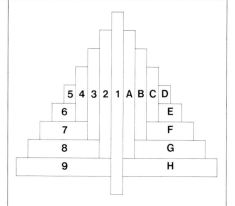

Machine-appliqué pieces to the towel with satin stitches.

Stitch ribbons in place and tie into bows; trim ends. Stitch pom-pom in place; embroider Santa's eyebrows.

## Patchwork Table Runner

Shown on page 37.

Finished size is approximately 17x69 inches.

### MATERIALS

1¾ yards of white fabric (1 yard for backing)
⅝ yard of three different red prints
⅝ yard of two different green prints
⅜ yard of red and green print on white background
¼ yard *each* of red and green solid-color fabrics
1 yard of lightweight quilt batting
Sewing and quilting threads
Embroidery floss
Graph paper

### INSTRUCTIONS

Preshrink all fabrics. Use ¼-inch seams throughout.

#### For the quilt squares

Draw 12-inch squares on graph paper. Draw in lines as directed on page 45 for each pattern. For each pattern piece cut a template, adding a ¼-inch seam allowance all around.

WATER WHEEL: Refer to drawing, *opposite.* On graph paper,

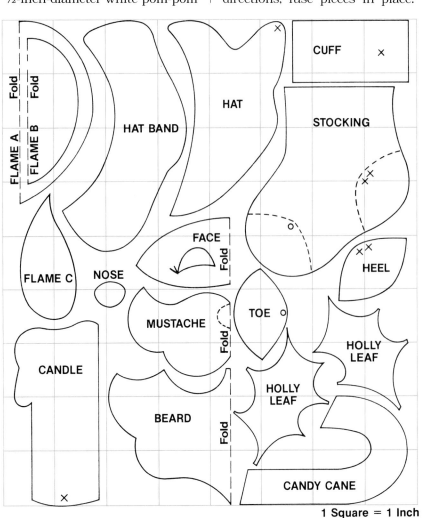

1 Square = 1 Inch

draw a 2-inch square (6 and 2), and a 4-inch square. Cut the 4-inch square in half diagonally for triangle pattern (7 and 9), adding seam allowances to each piece. Cut out templates.

Cut pieces from fabrics as indicated on diagram, *below right.*

Stitch triangles 7 and 9 together to form larger squares. Stitch squares 6 and 2 together to form larger squares. Arrange squares as indicated. Stitch squares into rows; stitch rows into block.

BIRD: Enlarge pattern, *below,* and make templates for heart, leaf, bird, and wing. Cut patterns from fabrics (see photo, page 37, for colors).

Cut a 12½-inch white square and position pattern pieces as shown in diagram. Hand-appliqué pieces into place. Embroider stems and bird's eye.

LOG CABIN FOUR-PATCH: Refer to diagram, *right,* and cut four 2½-inch red squares for centers. Cut 1½-inch strips of white (2), green print (7), and red print (4). *Note:* A ¼-inch seam allowance is included in these measurements. Piece each square as shown in diagram. Stitch squares together to form block.

VARIABLE STAR: Refer to pattern, *right,* and draw onto graph paper two 4-inch squares. Draw an X on one square, dividing it into four triangles; cut apart and use one triangle for pattern piece. Add seams; cut templates.

Cut pieces from fabrics as indicated in drawing and color key, *right.* Stitch triangles 3, 5, and 9

together to form squares. Refer to drawing for assembly.

BEAR'S PAW: See the pattern, *below,* and make the following templates: 3½-inch square, two 1¾-inch squares, one ½-inch square, and a 1½x5-inch rectangle. Cut one 1¾-inch square in half diagonally for triangle pattern. Add seams; cut pieces from fabrics. Sew triangles 5 and 9 together to form squares. Refer to drawing for assembly.

**Assembly**

Align the pieced squares side by side as desired.

From solid-color green fabric, cut four 1½x12½-inch sashing strips, two 1½x14-inch end border strips, and four 1½x64½-inch side border strips. From white print, cut two 1x14½-inch strips and two 1x67½-inch strips. *Note:* Long strips will have to be pieced.

Sew a green sashing strip between each of the finished quilt blocks.

Stitch a green side border strip to each long edge of the panel. Stitch the green end border strips to the ends of the panel. Sew white print border strips to the green strips.

Cut batting to measure 14x66 inches. Cut and piece backing fabric from white fabric to measure 18x70 inches.

Center and layer the three pieces; baste together and quilt as desired (omit quilting on the borders). Trim the backing to the size of the pieced top. Press under raw edge of backing ¼ inch. Set aside.

**For prairie point edging**

Draw a 2½-inch square for the master pattern. Cut a total of 96 squares from three different red prints (32 of each fabric). Fold each square in half diagonally, *continued*

## BIRD

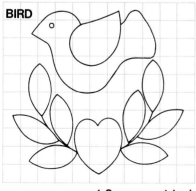

1 Square = 1 Inch

## BEAR'S PAW

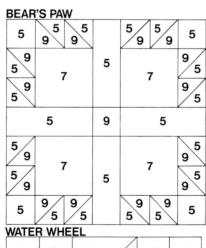

## LOG CABIN FOUR-PATCH

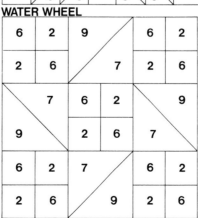

## WATER WHEEL

## VARIABLE STAR

## COLOR KEY

| | | |
|---|---|---|
| 1. Red | 4. Red Print | 7. Green Print |
| 2. White | 5. Red Dot | 8. Green Print |
| 3. Green | 6. Red Print | 9. White Print |

then in half diagonally again, and press. *Note:* Raw edge of fabric should measure 2½ inches.

Lay runner panel out right side up. Position points along the edge of the pieced panel, with the raw edges aligned (pointing away from edge).

Alternate the prints; use eight points along each short side and 40 points along each long side. Sew through the pieced top border only, ¼ inch from the edge. Turn under seam allowances of points and top; press. Slip-stitch backing to wrong side of points.

# Log Cabin
# Place Mats

Shown on page 36.

Finished size is 15x18 inches.

### MATERIALS
*(For four place mats)*
½ yard of fabric, pieced from three green print fabrics
1 yard of white cotton fabric (place mat fronts and backs)
½ yard of red print fabric for binding and tree ornaments
Four 15x18-inch rectangles of fleece
Matching sewing thread

### INSTRUCTIONS

#### Cutting the fabrics
Measurements include ¼-inch seams, unless otherwise noted.

PLACE MAT AND BINDING STRIPS: *For each* place mat, cut two 16x19-inch rectangles from white fabric, a matching shape from fleece, and two 1½x16-inch and two 1½x19-inch binding strips from red print fabric.

TREE: Cut green print fabrics into long strips (strips should be no wider than 2¾ inches, but widths *may* vary). Piece fabrics into new yardage. From this pieced fabric, cut two 1⅝-inch-wide strips in *each* of the following lengths (strips are cut parallel to pieced yardage strips): 6½ inches (H, 9); 5 inches (G, 8); 3½ inches (F, 7); and 2 inches (E, 6). Cut two 1¼-inch-wide strips in *each* of the following lengths: 8½ inches (A, 2); 6¼ inches (B, 3); 4 inches (C, 4); 1⅝ inches (D, 5); and one 11¾-inch (A) length.

From remaining red print, cut ¾-inch squares (includes ⅛-inch seams) for tree ornaments.

#### Appliquéing the tree
Baste fleece to wrong side of one white rectangle.
*Note:* When basting the pieced strips of the tree in place, baste down the *center* of the strips only.
Refer to assembly diagram on page 44. Press under seams on

Strip 1. Position Strip 1 in the center of the place mat; baste the strip in place.

For Strips 2–9, press under the *top* and *outside* seam allowance only. Repeat for Strips A–H.

Place raw edge of Strip 2 under Strip 1, 1⅛ inches from the top of Strip 1; baste Strip 2 in place. Place raw edge of Strip 3 under Strip 2, 1⅛ inches from top of Strip 2; baste in place. Repeat for Strips 4 and 5. Repeat the above procedure for Strips A–D.

Place Strip 6 atop Strip 5, positioning raw edge *under* Strip 4; baste in place. Repeat for Strips 7–9. Repeat this procedure for Strips E–H.

Topstitch all pieces in place.

Turn under raw edges on red squares and position at random; stitch in place. Remove basting.

#### Assembling the place mat
Baste backing to top, wrong sides facing. Quilt front and back together (see photograph). Finish edges with binding.

# Lath Barn
# Landscape

Shown on page 39.

### MATERIALS
Bundle of white pine lath
⅜-inch plywood
Jigsaw
Red, white, green, and black acrylic paints
Butcher and tracing papers
Sandpaper

### INSTRUCTIONS
Enlarge design, *left*, onto brown paper for a master pattern. Trace all shapes onto tracing paper and cut out. Number tracing paper pieces and master pattern for reference. Trace around each pattern piece onto wood lath.

Cut each pattern piece from lath. Sand lightly, if necessary. Paint pieces with a diluted solution of acrylics, using photograph as a guide for colors. Cut plywood to size of master pattern. Glue pieces to plywood backing. Frame as desired.

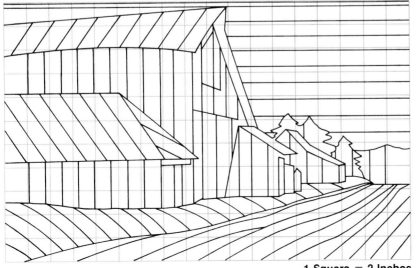

1 Square = 2 Inches

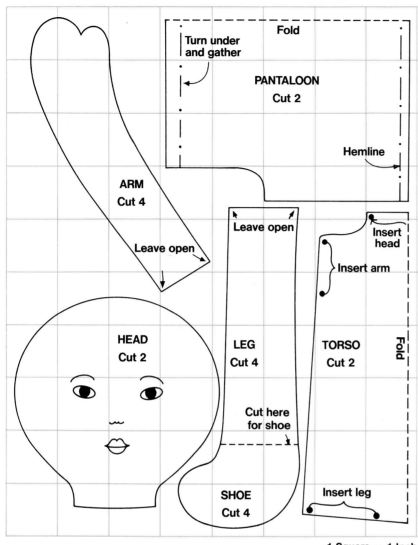

**Turn under and gather**

**Fold**

**PANTALOON**
Cut 2

**Hemline**

**ARM**
Cut 4

**Leave open**

**Leave open**

**Insert head**

**Insert arm**

**HEAD**
Cut 2

**LEG**
Cut 4

**TORSO**
Cut 2

**Fold**

**Cut here for shoe**

**SHOE**
Cut 4

**Insert leg**

1 Square = 1 Inch

## Patchwork Tablecloth

Shown on page 38.

**MATERIALS**
41-inch red print square
Four 11-inch red squares (corners)
Forty 5x11-inch rectangles in various red and green prints
8 yards of red bias tape

**INSTRUCTIONS**
Using ½-inch seams, sew 10 rectangles together randomly for each border strip.

Attach one red corner piece to end of each strip. Pin strips to red print square so each corner piece extends from corner of center fabric. Sew, using a ½-inch seam. Bind edges with bias tape.

## Dishcloth Dolls

Shown on page 39.

Finished size is about 13 inches tall.

**MATERIALS**
*(For one doll)*
¼ yard of muslin (body, pantaloons); one dishcloth (dress)
Scrap of striped fabric (shoes)
Scraps of lace (pantaloon and arm trims); two small buttons
Embroidery floss (features)
Novelty yarn (hair); fiberfill

**INSTRUCTIONS**
Enlarge pattern, *above*, onto kraft paper; cut out.

For smaller dolls, change the number of inches each square on the grid represents. For example,

instead of 1 square equaling 1 inch of the grid, make 1 square represent ¾ inch.

*Note:* Pattern pieces include ¼-inch seam allowances.

Transfer all of the patterns, except shoes, to muslin.

Do not cut out head until the face is embroidered. Use satin, outline, and straight stitches in the colors of your choice to embroider facial features.

Cut out pattern pieces and a ½x2-inch rectangle (wig strip) from muslin.

Cut shoes from striped fabric.

**Assembling the doll body**
Sew shoes to legs.

Stitch arm and leg sets together, leaving openings at the tops for turning. With right sides facing, sew torso together, leaving 2 inches at the top of the side seams unstitched and an opening at the bottom for turning. Clip curves, turn to the right side, and press.

Stuff the arms and legs with fiberfill. Sew arms to side openings in torso, then stuff torso.

Press under raw edges at bottom of torso; insert legs and topstitch opening closed.

HAIR: Cut yarn into strands the desired length of hair. Cut enough to cover length of wig strip. Center yarn over wig strip and stitch down the center forming a part. Braid into pigtails, form into loops at side of head, or twist into a bun.

**Assembling clothing**
PANTALOONS: Sew the curved front and back seams; sew inseam. Clip curves, turn to right side, and press.

Hem pantaloon legs; trim with lace. Turn under waistline, slip onto doll, and gather to fit. Slipstitch to doll.

JUMPER: Overlap the edges of the dishcloth; topstitch together, forming a cylinder shape. Slip over doll with overlapped edges in back. Gather top edge to fit.

Hem jumper. Attach straps, cut from scraps of cloth. Sew buttons to straps. Trim arms with lace.

# CROSS-STITCHED SAMPLER

Christmas roses, poinsettias, and trees bedecked with candles frame the holiday sampler, *right*.

Use the many motifs in this design to create an assortment of gifts for family and friends. Trim a basket with the cross-stitched border design or work selected motifs on a warm wool scarf or knitted gauntlets. Turn the page for ornaments using the motifs and for all instructions.

# Christmas Sampler

Finished size is 17x21 inches.

## MATERIALS
25x29 inches of ecru hardanger
Embroidery floss (see color key)
Embroidery hoop and needle
Graph paper; felt-tip pens

## INSTRUCTIONS
Using felt-tip pens, chart the pattern, pages 52–53, onto graph paper. "Flop" (make mirror images of) some of the motifs to complete the pattern.

Flop pattern to left of dashed line. *Note:* Pear tree and saying are complete. Repeat motifs A, B, and C as indicated. Add alphabet, page 53, to pattern using Xs at bottom of diagram as placement guides. Finish lower border, flopping motifs above dashed line.

Hem fabric edges to prevent raveling. Work stitches with two strands of floss over two fabric threads. Measure 4 inches down and 4 inches in from upper left corner of fabric; mark with a pin. Begin stitching here.

Work top stitch of every cross-stitch in the same direction. Begin stitching with green border.

When all stitching is complete, remove tape, press, and frame.

# Gauntlet Gloves

Directions are for one size, which will fit Sizes 6½, 7, and 7½.

## MATERIALS
Coats & Clark Red Heart 4-ply hand knitting yarn: 7 ounces of No. 3 off-white
Size 6 double-pointed needles, or size to obtain gauge, *below*
Size G aluminum crochet hook
Coats & Clark Red Heart Persian-type yarn: 1 skein *each* of red, coral, and dark green; tapestry needle

**Abbreviations:** See page 53.
**Gauge:** Over st st, 5 sts = 1 inch; 7 rnds = 1 inch.

## INSTRUCTIONS

### Left glove
Beg at cuff, cast on 72 sts. Divide sts among 3 needles, with 24 sts on each. Join, being careful not to twist sts. *Rnd 1:* * K 1, p 1. Rep from * around. Change to st st (k each rnd) until length measures 3½ inches. *Dec rnd 1:* Dec 4 sts evenly spaced, k around—68 sts. Work even for 7 rnds.

*Dec rnd 2:* K around, dec 4 sts evenly spaced. Work even for 7 rnds. Rep last 8 rnds twice more—56 sts.

*Next dec rnd:* * K 1, (k 2 tog) twice. Rep from * to last st, k 1—34 sts. *Next 4 rnds:* Work in k 1, p 1 ribbing. Work in st st for 7 rnds. Mark end of rnd.

*Thumb gore—Rnd 1:* K 16, place a marker on needle, inc 1 st in each of next 2 sts, place another marker on needle, k 16. *Rnd 2:* Sl markers, k around. *Rnd 3:* K to 1st marker, sl marker, inc 1 st in next st, k to 1 st before next marker, inc 1 st in next st, sl marker, k rem sts. Rep last 2 rnds alternately 3 times—12 sts bet markers. *Next rnd:* K to 1st marker, remove marker, sl next 12 thumb gore sts to holder, remove next marker, cast on 2 sts, k 16—34 sts. Continuing in st st until 2 cast-on sts are 2 inches.

*Index finger—Rnd 1:* K 12, sl these sts to another holder and mark for palm section, k next 10 sts, cast on 2 sts, sl rem sts to another holder for back section, having point of holder facing finger. Divide 12 sts among 3 needles for index finger. Work in st st until length of finger is 2½ inches. *Last rnd:* * K 2 tog. Rep from * around. Leaving a 6-inch tail, break off. Draw tail tightly through rem sts and secure.

*Middle finger:* Sl next 4 sts from back section onto needle, sl the 4 corresponding sts from

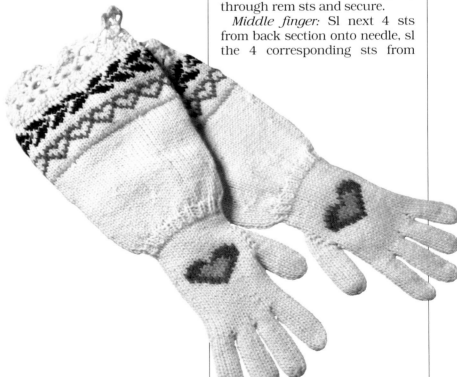

palm section onto another needle. *Rnd 1:* Pick up and k 2 sts along base of previous finger bet back and palm sections, k next 4 sts, with another needle cast on 2 sts, k next 4 sts. Divide the 12 sts evenly among 3 needles and work in st st until length of finger is 2¾ inches. Beg with last rnd, complete as for Index Finger.

*Ring finger:* Work as for Middle Finger until length is 2½ inches. Complete as for Middle Finger.

*Little finger:* Sl sts from holder onto needles as for Middle Finger. *Rnd 1:* Pick up and k 3 sts along base of previous finger, k rem 8 sts. Work as for previous finger over the 11 sts until length is 2¼ inches. Complete as for previous finger.

*Thumb:* Sl sts from holder onto 3 needles, pick up and k 2 sts along the 2 cast-on sts at base—14 sts. Work as for previous finger until length is 2¼ inches. Complete as for previous finger.

### Crocheted edging

With crochet hook and off-white, ch 4. *Row 1:* In 4th ch from hook make *3 dc, ch 3, and 3 dc*—shell made; ch 3, turn. *Row 2:* Make shell in sp of next shell; ch 3, turn. *Row 3:* Make shell in sp of next shell, ch 5, turn. *Row 4:* Rep Row 2. *Row 5:* Shell in sp of next shell, ch 2, in next ch-5 turning ch lp on this side of edging make (dc, ch 2) 5 times and dc; sc in next ch-3 turning ch lp on same side of edging; ch 3, turn.

*Row 6:* Make 2 dc in 1st ch-2 sp; (in next ch-2 sp make sl st, ch 3, and 2 dc) 4 times; sc in next ch-2 sp, ch 3, shell in sp of next shell; ch 3, turn. Rep Rows 3–6 four times—5 scallops along long edge of edging. Fasten off.

Sew first shell to last shell, then sew edge without scallops to cast-on sts of cuff.

### Right glove

Work as for Left Glove with changes as follow.

*Middle finger—Rnd 1:* Cast on 2 sts, pick up and k 4 from palm section, pick up and k 2 along the base of the previous finger bet back and palm sections, k 4 from the back section.

*Little finger—Rnd 1:* Pick up and k 4 sts from palm section, pick up and k 3 sts along base of previous finger, k 4.

### Embroidery

Select motifs from the diagram, page 52, to trim gloves. See photographs for inspiration. *Note:* Because the gloves are worked in rounds, border patterns will not meet on the back side.

Determine the center front of each glove; begin the decorative stitching here. Work motifs using cross-stitches or duplicate stitches as pictured. Use one yarn strand for stitching.

# Sampler Ornaments

### MATERIALS

25-count evenweave linen
Embroidery floss (see color key)
½-inch-wide lace for edging
Polyester fleece (stuffing)
Embroidery hoop and needle
Graph paper; felt-tip pens

### INSTRUCTIONS

Select motifs from diagram on page 52. The ornaments pictured use motifs from sampler border.

Chart designs on graph paper using felt-tip pens.

Use three strands of floss for working cross-stitches. Tape fabric edges to prevent raveling.

Work each stitch over four fabric threads. Leave enough fabric between motifs to cut out desired shapes. Do not cut out ornaments until embroidery is completed.

Draw patterns as follow: 3x4½-inch oval (tree), 4x4½-inch heart (poinsettia), and 3-inch-diameter circle (Christmas rose). Seams are *not* included.

Center patterns atop stitched motifs. Draw around outline; cut out, adding ¼-inch seams. Cut a matching back and two shapes from fleece for each ornament.

Baste fleece to wrong side of front and back. Baste lace to ornament front. With right sides facing, sew front to back, leaving an opening. Turn and sew opening. Add ribbon loop for hanging.
*continued*

1 Square = 1 Cross-stitch

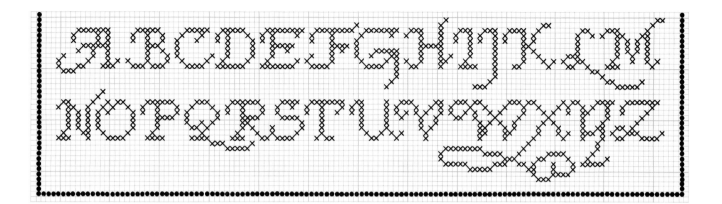

## Sampler Scarf

Finished size is 9¼x48 inches, including the fringe.

**MATERIALS**
15x54-inch piece of off-white Pendelton wool fabric
⅓ yard of off-white lining fabric
Two 10x10-inch pieces of 10-count waste canvas
Embroidery floss (see color key)
Graph paper (10 squares to the inch); felt-tip markers
Embroidery hoop and needle

**INSTRUCTIONS**
Draw two 9¼x9¼-inch squares on graph paper (one for each end of the scarf). Refer to the photograph on page 51 for inspiration and the sampler chart, *opposite*, for design motifs; chart designs, as desired, using felt-tip pens. *Note:* Do *not* chart symbols to the edges of the squares; leave a ½-inch *uncharted* area around the *inside* of each square.

Using a water-soluble marker, draw a 9¼x48-inch rectangle on the wool fabric and add a ½-inch seam allowance along *long sides only;* sew basting stitches atop these lines.

Baste a piece of waste canvas to each end of the wool, carefully *centering* the canvas on the fabric and placing it with the straight grain of the fabric. Position the canvas *3 inches from each end* of the rectangle to allow for fringe.

Separate the floss and use three strands to work cross-stitches.

Place the fabric in the hoop. Pull needle through *tiniest* holes on waste canvas. Be careful not to catch the waste canvas as you stitch; otherwise, removing canvas threads is difficult.
*Note:* Work designs so they appear right side up when worn.

Lightly moisten the waste canvas and pull out the threads; press embroidery. Cut out scarf ½ inch from seam line along the *long sides* and along the width. Fringe scarf by pulling threads at each end for 3 inches; set aside.

Cut lining to measure 10¼x43 inches (includes ½-inch seams).

With *right* sides facing, sew lengthwise seams. Turn scarf to right side. Press under ½ inch on lining and sew lining to scarf.

## Basket Ruffle

**MATERIALS**
Purchased woven basket
25-count even-weave fabric 9 inches wide and 1⅓ times the basket diameter
Embroidery floss (see color key)
Embroidery hoop and needle
¼-inch elastic, 2 inches shorter than basket diameter
Graph paper
Felt-tip markers

**INSTRUCTIONS**
Use border, minus holly leaves, *opposite*, for ruffle design.

Fold the fabric in half length-wise; mark this center line using a water-soluble pen.

Use two strands of embroidery floss to work cross-stitches.

Work design on upper half of fabric length, ¾ inch above center line. Work stitches over two fabric threads. Begin stitching in center of ruffle and work to ends. Finish each end with border motif in upper right corner of diagram.

Press. Hem short ends; fold strip in half lengthwise, right sides facing. Sew long edge, using ½-inch seam; turn.

Sew ½-inch-wide casing 1 inch from top of ruffle. Insert elastic; adjust to fit basket. Join ends to form circle. Place on basket.

## Knit and Crochet Abbreviations

| | |
|---|---|
| beg | begin(ning) |
| bet | between |
| ch | chain |
| dc | double crochet |
| dec | decrease |
| grp | group |
| hdc | half-double crochet |
| inc | increase |
| k | knit |
| lp(s) | loop(s) |
| p | purl |
| rem | remaining |
| rep | repeat |
| rnd | round |
| sc | single crochet |
| sk | skip |
| sl st | slip stitch |
| sp | space |
| st(s) | stitch(es) |
| st st | stockinette stitch |
| tog | together |
| trc | treble crochet |
| yo | yarn over |
| * | repeat from * as indicated |

# Holiday Treats for Children

Christmastime is a wondrous occasion for all, but to children it becomes an adventure of magical times alive with excitement and anticipation.

Craft special treats for your little ones to ensure happy times and wonderful memories. In this section you'll find extraordinary things for Christmas fun.

Stockings to hang, an advent tree to fill with tiny gifts, whimsical Santa and reindeer dolls, and special holiday outfits are just part of the excitement.

Begin the good times with a pint-sized tree decorated in a toyland theme. Soldiers on horseback and marching band members make up the Christmas parade— complete with beribboned whistles for tots to toot. Instructions for these projects begin on page 64.

**L**ittle helpers will love these wonderful handmades. Crafted with Christmas fun in mind, each depicts a stylized interpretation of the Silent Night theme.

A wintry night scene of snow-covered trees and shining stars, set against a subtly variegated midnight blue sky, is shown on a toddler's knitted pullover vest, *opposite*.

Stitch up the patterned vest in no time at all for the little ones on your gift list.

**W**ith childlike simplicity, the Silent Night theme is repeated on the embroidered jumper *at right*.

Stitch the winter landscape onto white fabric—a snowy village nestles in embroidered valleys, colored lights decorate the Christmas trees, and stars twinkle in the heavens above.

Then appliqué the rolling hills to the front of a commercial pattern.

Even a beginner can work the design in time for Christmas giving, since it's embellished with easy-to-embroider satin, outline, and French-knot stitches.

# HOLIDAY TREATS FOR CHILDREN

Waking up and finding a stocking brimming with treasures is one of the fondest childhood memories. And what a delight to discover one of these cheery machine-appliquéd stockings, shown *at right,* on Christmas morning.

Each has a special place for an extra holiday treat. Festive goose, teddy bear, and holiday house motifs hide a tiny front pocket for a secret gift.

The design shapes are cut from colorful prints and stitched onto a stocking large enough to hold lots of Christmas goodies inside.

Patterns and instructions for creating these stockings begin on page 64.

Another part of Christmas magic for children is discovering all sorts of wished-for toys and packages under the tree. Just imagine a child finding something unexpected like the Santa Claus doll and reindeer shown *opposite.*

Craft the 18-inch-tall likeness of the jolly old elf as an extra-special Christmas treat, a whimsical decoration for your home, or a holiday centerpiece. However you use them, Santa and his reindeer friend are certain to become an instant Christmas tradition.

These endearing toys are stitched from muslin, white felt, and pinwale corduroy. Embroidered features, Santa's quilted beard, and shiny, bright jingle bells are the finishing touches on these seasonal soft sculptures.

And what Santa would be complete without a bag full of gifts and goodies?

Santa's pack, shown *opposite,* below right, is made from squares of pinwale corduroy and lined with a bright Christmas print.

For picture-perfect results, fill it with candies, miniatures, and tiny wrapped packages.

Little girls have an angelic way about them, especially at Christmastime.

This Christmas, give your little angel a special holiday treat with her own angel wall plaque, *left,* to hang in her room. This glorious decoration is a wonderful surprise, and sure to become a holiday treasure.

Paint this 24x44-inch design on muslin in soft pastels, then embroider the outlines and details. Appliqué stars and the robe trim using a pastel print for added effect.

Or, stitch and stuff a miniature band of heavenly angels, *below.* Attach ribbon loops and tie them on the tree or onto Christmas gifts for unique package decorations. Or, fill them with potpourri to make sweetly scented sachets.

The design is painted onto muslin first, and then embroidered and embellished with beads and metallic thread for holiday sparkle. Simple zigzag stitching, using metallic threads, outlines the ornaments' shapes.

You will find a full-size pattern on page 71 to make these 7-inch-tall figures.

Tiny angels herald the coming of Christmas Day on the cross-stitched stocking, *opposite.*

A masterful work of patience and love, it is destined to become a cherished heirloom.

Rows of ribbons, hearts, and tiny flowers add to the design of this especially delicate stitchery.

Work the motifs in subtle peaches, pink, rose, and green on ecru hardanger fabric. Trim the stocking with antique and purchased laces, metallic threads, beads, and narrow satin ribbons for a soft and feminine feel, befitting a little girl.

# HOLIDAY TREATS FOR CHILDREN

Looking for an unforgettable holiday treat to give to a special little girl? This gingham skirt, *opposite,* with its cross-stitched Christmas tree border and bright red crocheted trim fills the bill. She's sure to look forward to all the season's parties and pageants when she can wear this enchanting Christmas outfit.

Work the festive border design along one edge of the fabric and in a twinkling you can stitch up the skirt with the ruffled and double-elasticized waist for a daughter, niece, granddaughter, or favorite little person.

Christmas morning, with all its magic and wonder, is perhaps one of the most spellbinding times in a young child's life.

Eyes will open wide in surprise and excitement when youngsters see this fabric and eyelet tree, *above,* filled with lots of miniature gifts and candy treats. (Five rows of tiny pockets around the tree hold each treasure until discovery.)

Make the tree for Santa Claus to fill and little ones to find on Christmas morning. Or use the decorative soft sculpture as an Advent decoration. Fill each pocket with a little wrapped package—one for each day until Christmas morning arrives.

(For another look at the crocheted pastel snowflakes shown in the window, see page 7. Instructions begin on page 15. Turn to page 39 for a close-up of the doll and page 47 for pattern and complete instructions.)

## Soldier Ornaments

Shown on page 55.

Finished size is 7 inches tall.

**MATERIALS**
Aluminum tooling foil
Orange sticks
Tissue paper
Permanent felt-tip markers (in colors of your choice)
Monofilament thread
Plastic spoon; scissors

**INSTRUCTIONS**
Enlarge the patterns, *opposite*, onto heavy tissue paper; cut out.
Lay patterns atop foil; transfer lines with a pencil onto foil, pushing firmly. Push down foil at dark gray areas on diagram using an orange stick; cut out soldiers using scissors. Turn soldiers over; push down foil at light gray areas on diagram. Rework the lines on the front.
Flatten outside edges with a spoon. Color soldiers using markers. Poke hole through foil; thread with monofilament for hanging.

## Embroidered Snow Scene Jumper

Shown on page 57.

**MATERIALS**
Commercial jumper pattern
Dark blue fabric (yardage as specified in pattern)
¾ yard of white cotton fabric (snow-covered hills)
Embroidery floss in the following colors: red, yellow, green, blue, white, light blue, light green, brown, and gray
Water-soluble marking pen

**INSTRUCTIONS**
Cut pattern pieces from blue fabric. Enlarge design on page 66 onto paper.

**Transferring the design**
Transfer the snow-covered hills area of design onto white fabric with marker; adjust design to fit jumper front. Appliqué this piece

to jumper; baste along seam lines. Transfer sky design to blue area of jumper front.

**Embroidering the design**
Work the design, except for tree lights, in outline or backstitches.

SNOW-COVERED HILLS: Outline hills with light blue, Christmas trees with greens, trees with brown, buildings and smoke with gray, roofs with red or blue, snowman with light blue, and hat with blue. Work brown seed stitches for snowman features. Satin-stitch tree lights in a variety of colors. Work French knots on tiny trees in different colors.

SKY: Outline clouds with white. Work yellow French knots and long stitches for stars.

**Jumper assembly**
Stitch jumper following commercial pattern instructions.

## Silent Night Child's Vest

Shown on page 56.

Directions are for Size Small (3) (changes for Size Medium (6) and Size Large (8) follow in parentheses). Chest = 22 (24, 26) inches.

**MATERIALS**
Manos Strya handspun yarn (100-gram skeins): 1 (1, 2) skeins white, 1 (1, 2) skeins blue; 3 yards yellow
Sizes 7 and 10 knitting needles, or size to obtain gauge below
Size H aluminum crochet hook

**Abbreviations:** See page 53.
**Gauge:** With the larger needles over st st, 4 sts = 1 inch; 5 rows = 1 inch.

**INSTRUCTIONS**
*Note on 2-color knitting:* When changing yarn colors, twist new color around color in use to prevent making holes. Carry unused yarn loosely across back of work, twisting it around yarn in use every three or four stitches.

FRONT: With the smaller needles and white, cast on 44 (48, 52) sts. Work in k 1, p 1 ribbing for 2 inches. Change to the larger needles and work 12 (16, 20) rows st st, then work from chart on page 67 for 20 (22, 24) rows.

ARMHOLE SHAPING: Cast off 3 sts at beg of next 2 rows. Dec 1 st each end every other row twice—34 (38, 42) sts. Work even until final row of chart. *Last row:* K 8 (9, 10) and sl to holder for shoulder, cast off center 18 (20, 22) sts, k to end of row, sl sts to holder for shoulder.

BACK: With blue only, work as for Front until 12 (12, 14) rows past beg of armhole shaping. K 11 (13, 14), cast off center 12 (12, 14) sts, k to end of row. Working on right shoulder only, dec 1 st at neck edge every other row 3 (4, 4) times—8 (9, 10) sts. Attach yarn to left shoulder and finish as for right, reversing shaping.

**Finishing**
Weave shoulder sts tog. Sew side seams. With blue and the right side facing, work two rows of sc around the neck and armhole edges. Fasten off.

## Santa Doll

Shown on page 59.

Finished size is 18 inches tall.

**MATERIALS**
**Body and face**
½ yard of unbleached muslin
1¾x2¾-inch piece of white bonded mending tape
Two 9x12-inch pieces of white felt; red and black felt scraps
Black floss; powdered rouge
Polyester fiberfill
**Santa suit**
¾ yard of red baby-wale corduroy
1 yard of ¼-inch-wide elastic
⅛ yard of white fur fabric
1-inch-diameter white pom-pom
Scrap of green T-shirt fabric
¼ yard of black suede fabric
Gold belt buckle; snap

## Gift bag

⅓ yard of green wide-wale corduroy
⅓ yard of green dotted fabric
2 yards of ⅝-inch-wide green satin ribbon
Four ½-inch-diameter bells

## INSTRUCTIONS

Enlarge pattern, page 70, onto paper. Cut head, legs, arms, body fronts and backs, and a 2-inch-diameter circle for nose from muslin. From red, cut jacket fronts and back, two 9¼x10½-inch rectangles for the trousers, and an 11¾x13-inch rectangle for the hat. Place pieces so nap is in same direction.

Cut beard, mustache, and hair from white felt; use red felt for mouth. Cut boot pieces from black suede fabric. Cut mittens from green knit.

From white fur cut a 3¾x13-inch strip for hat trim, a ½x20-inch strip for jacket trim, and two cuffs measuring 1¾x5 inches.

For bag, cut two 9½x10¼-inch rectangles *each* from corduroy and dotted fabric. For belt, cut a 2x16-inch strip of black suede fabric and two 5¼x6½-inch boot cuffs.

### Assembling the doll

BODY: Use ¼-inch seams unless otherwise noted. Stitch all the doll body seams twice, using small stitches for strength.

With right sides facing, stitch the body fronts together; repeat for the body backs. Stitch front to back at sides and bottom. Clip the curves and turn to the right side.

Stuff body and neck *very firmly* using the eraser end of a pencil to assist; stitch neck opening closed.

HEAD: Bond mending tape following manufacturer's directions to wrong side of one headpiece. Cut a 1½-inch opening through center of tape. With right sides facing, sew heads together. Clip curves, turn, and stuff firmly.

Insert neck into head opening, forcing neck as needed into a natural position; pin together with T pins. Use a double strand of thread to join head and neck at opening and under chin.

LEGS AND ARMS: Sew legs together with right sides facing. Trim seam at toe to ⅛ inch; clip curves and turn. Stuff firmly, using less stuffing at top. Match center seams and sew top closed. Sew legs to body. Repeat for arms.

FACIAL FEATURES: For nose, make gathering stitches at outer edges of muslin circle. Place a ball of fiberfill in center and pull gathers tight. Tie off threads and trim excess fabric. Flatten nose; sew to face 2 inches from chin. Powder with rouge.

Cut eyes from black felt; pin to face. Using two strands of black floss, work satin stitches over each eye and straight stitches for eyelashes. Make highlights with white thread. Brush cheeks with rouge.

Sew beard pieces around outer edges, leaving opening for turning. Clip curves; trim seam close to stitching; turn and stuff lightly. Stitch opening closed; topstitch along stitching lines (use inside lines of beard pattern as a guide). Stitch long swirl at beard center.

Pin beard to face. Hand-sew along top of beard. Sew top of mouth to center top of beard.

Finish mustache and hair like beard. Topstitch mustache; position and stitch atop beard. Sew hair to back of head, matching top corners of hair and beard.

### Assembling the clothing

TROUSERS: With the right sides facing, sew corduroy pieces together at long edge for 5½ inches; press seams. Align seams and pin each inside leg; sew, beginning at bottom of center seam.

**1 Square = 1 Inch**

*continued*

For waist and leg casings, press under ¼ inch and then ⅜ inch at edges. Sew along inside fold, leaving opening for elastic. Insert the elastic; overlap ends and tack. Sew casings closed.

JACKET: Press under ¼ inch at center front edge and sew. Sew back to fronts, right sides facing, along sleeve tops; press. Hem the neck edge. Sew back to fronts at undersleeves and sides. Make the sleeve casings; insert elastic.

To trim jacket with fur, turn under ends of jacket trim and sew in half lengthwise with wrong sides facing. Pin to bottom of jacket, ending ½ inch from ends. Fold ends of jacket over fur and sew. Folds ends in at top and stitch at bottom; press. Sew snap to neck top. Repeat for cuffs.

BELT: Sew piece in half lengthwise, leaving opening in center for turning. Turn and stitch the opening. Attach buckle.

BOOTS: Sew dart at toe of upper; press. Sew boot cuff to edge of upper; clip curves and press. Sew center back together. Stitch sole to upper; trim seam to ⅛ inch. Fold cuff to inside and tack.

MITTENS: Sew together with ⅛-inch seams, leaving top open. Trim the seams, clip curves, and turn. Hem raw edge at cuff.

HAT: Sew short sides of piece, right sides facing. Gather end and tie off; attach pom-pom. Sew fur into tube, right sides facing. Fold fur in half, wrong sides facing; sew raw edges together. Slip hat inside tube, sew, and turn; turn fur up as cuff. Tack to head.

### Assembling the gift bag

Sew bag pieces together, leaving top open and a ¾-inch opening in sides 3 inches from top for ribbon. Sew lining together. Sew lining to bag with right sides facing, matching seams and raw edges. Turn; fold under lining raw edges and topstitch. Fold lining to inside of bag.

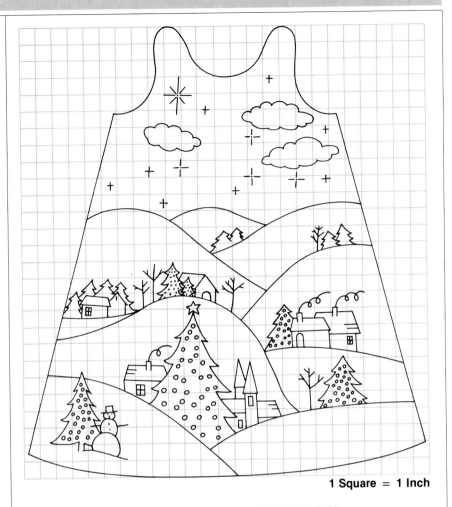

**1 Square = 1 Inch**

For the casing, topstitch at either side of openings in sides. Pull ribbons through casings and attach bells; tie bows at sides of bag.

## Reindeer Toy

Shown on page 59.

Finished size is 18 inches.

### MATERIALS
⅔ yard of 45-inch-wide light brown baby-wale corduroy
⅛ yard of 45-inch-wide ivory baby-wale corduroy
⅓ yard of narrow bias tape or bias nylon seam finishing
Black embroidery floss
1 red and 2 white felt squares
Scraps of brown and tan felt
5 jingle bells
Powdered rouge
2 yards of ¼-inch-wide satin ribbon
Polyester fiberfill
Dressmaker's carbon

### INSTRUCTIONS
Enlarge the pattern pieces on page 70. Place each pattern piece on fabric with the nap running in the same direction.

Cut head gusset, body, and underbody pieces, tail, and ears from light brown corduroy. From ivory, cut the tail and inner ear pieces. From felt cut two brown eyes, two tan eyes, and one brown nose.

Transfer darts (dotted lines on chart) to wrong side of fabric with dressmaker's carbon.

Use ¼-inch seam allowances throughout. Stitch all of the body seams twice using small stitches for added strength. Finger-press all seams open.

BODY: With right sides facing, pin head gusset together lengthwise and stitch each dart; clip center of each dart. With right sides facing, pin gusset to one body piece; stitch together from B to C. Clip curves and press open. Repeat for remaining gusset side and body piece.

With right sides facing, pin the body backs together; sew from A to B. Pin chins together; sew from C to D. Clip curves; press.

With right sides facing, pin together and sew each underleg dart; clip center. Pin each underbody to matching body piece. Sew together from D to A. Clip curves; press open. With the right sides facing, pin and sew underbody pieces, leaving open between Xs. Clip curves, press, and turn.

To stuff, use the eraser end of a pencil to work stuffing into small areas. Stuff all areas *very firmly*. Stuff head; then stuff each leg. Stuff the body, adding additional fiberfill to head, neck, and legs as needed. Sew opening closed.

TAIL: Pin and stitch tails together with right sides facing, leaving small opening for turning. Turn and lightly stuff base of tail; sew opening closed. Gather tail's base slightly; sew to body.

EARS: Pin and stitch two pairs of each color together, leaving an opening for turning. Turn to the right side and sew the openings closed. With bases even, center ivory to brown; stitch together. Fold in half with ivory inside and sew to head at gusset seams.

EYES: Sew tan to dark brown circles. Use white thread for highlights. Sew to head; stuff slightly.

NOSE: Pin felt piece to head; sew around edges, stuffing slightly. Embroider the mouth with stem stitches or backstitches, using two strands of black floss. Color cheeks with rouge.

ANTLER: Pin antler pattern to white felt; trace around outline. Pin traced felt atop second piece of felt. Stitch together ⅛ inch inside the traced lines, using small stitches and leaving base open. Cut out following traced lines.

Stuff firmly using crochet hook to assist. Pin antlers in place and firmly sew base to head. Gently bend into natural position.

BELT: Pin pattern to felt and make as for antlers. Sew two rows of stitches ½ inch apart along center; attach bells. Sew ribbon to underside at one end; place belt on deer and tack other end to ribbon, fitting tightly.

Tie ribbons into bow around neck. Trim ribbon.

# Appliquéd Christmas Stockings

Shown on page 58.

Finished size is 15½ inches high.

## MATERIALS
½ yard of red calico for *each* stocking
½ yard of interfacing
Scraps of fusible webbing for appliqués
Calico scraps in various colors for appliqués (see the directions *at right*)
Scraps of ribbon and eyelet for goose design

## INSTRUCTIONS
*Note:* Use ¼ inch for seam allowances throughout, unless otherwise specified.

Enlarge the patterns for the stocking and cuff on page 69 onto paper.

Transfer stocking pattern onto red calico. Cut two stocking pieces (front and back) from *both* red calico fabric and interfacing.

Baste interfacing to the wrong side of the stocking pieces.

Cut the cuff and hanging loop from the following: *For the teddy bear stocking,* use white Christmas print; *for goose stocking,* use red-and-green plaid; *for Christmas cottage stocking,* use green calico fabric.

### Cutting out the appliqués
Enlarge the patterns for the appliqués, page 68, onto paper.

Without adding seams, cut out the appliqué pieces as directed on page 68.

TEDDY BEAR STOCKING: Cut the bear and two bear pockets from brown small-scale print, cut
*continued*

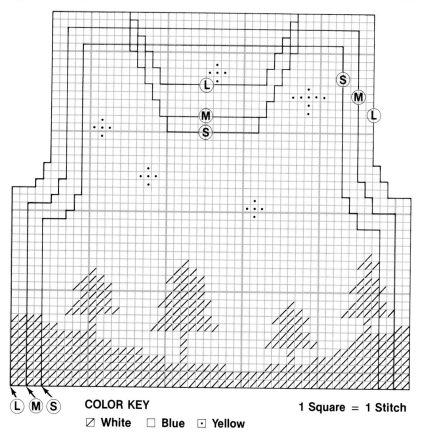

COLOR KEY     1 Square = 1 Stitch

☑ White    ☐ Blue    ⊡ Yellow

the balloon from white Christmas print (same as cuff), and cut the heart from red pindot fabric.

GOOSE STOCKING: Cut body and two wing pieces from solid white fabric, cut beak and feet from yellow calico, and cut the space between the feet from the same calico used for the stocking.

COTTAGE STOCKING: Cut cottage roof and door from green-and-white stripe, cut gable from green calico (same as cuff), cut the cottage front from red-on-white pindot, cut the cottage side from white Christmas print, cut window from yellow calico, and cut cottage tree from a different green calico.

### Appliquéing the shapes to the stockings

Cut out an identical piece of webbing for each appliqué.

Following the manufacturer's directions, affix the appliqué to the background fabric as directed *below.*

Using thread colors to match the appliqués (unless otherwise noted), machine-satin-stitch over raw edges of appliqué as follows.

TEDDY BEAR STOCKING: Appliqué heart to bear. Place the pocket pieces right sides together; stitch along the top edge only; turn to the right side and press. Place the pocket atop the bear body; trim raw edges so shapes are identical and then baste in place. Machine-embroider the facial details with white satin stitches. Using white thread, appliqué the bear and balloon to the stocking front; machine-stitch the balloon string. Tack small bow to neck.

GOOSE STOCKING: Pin and baste a small length of eyelet to right side of one wing (pocket) piece. Place both wing pieces to-

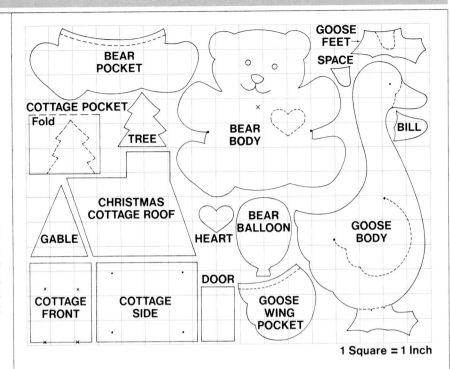

1 Square = 1 Inch

gether, right sides facing; stitch along top edge only, turn, and press.

Stuff wing lightly with polyester fiberfill and machine-satin-stitch to goose body. Using green thread, embroider a French knot eye. Appliqué goose body to stocking front. Affix red space between feet; affix feet and beak to goose. Add red-and-green-striped ribbon bow at neck.

COTTAGE STOCKING: Use green thread for appliquéing all pieces. Appliqué tree to one half of window (pocket). Fold in half and stitch to cottage side. Appliqué door to front. Appliqué the roof, gable, and house front and side to stocking.

### Assembling the stockings

Use ½-inch seams. With right sides together, stitch wide edge of one cuff to top of stocking front; turn and press. Repeat for stocking back. With right sides facing, stitch stocking front to back. Clip curves, turn, and press. Turn back cuff; blindstitch inner edge of cuff to inside of stocking.

For the hanging loop, fold the long edges of loop piece to the center; sew. Fold in half; tack to the stocking top.

# Musical Angel Wall Hanging and Ornaments

Shown on page 60.

Wall hanging is 28x44 inches. Ornaments are 8 inches tall.

### MATERIALS
### Wall hanging

1½ yards of muslin
⅓ yard of blue calico fabric
Quilt batting
Acrylic paints in yellow, pink, peach, blue, brown, and flesh
No. 5 DMC pearl cotton floss in colors darker than paint colors
Gold metallic thread
Paintbrush; dressmaker's carbon
26x42-inch piece of ¾-inch plywood

### Ornaments

Muslin
Acrylic paints in desired colors
Embroidery floss; beads
Silver and gold metallic threads in fine and medium widths
Fleece; polyester fiberfill
Dressmaker's carbon paper

## INSTRUCTIONS

### For the wall hanging

Enlarge pattern, page 71; transfer to muslin using carbon.

PAINTING: Mix paints with water to consistency of light cream.

Add a light wash of color to wings (yellow), hair (peach), robe (blue), dress (pink), shoes and violin (brown), and skin (flesh). *Note:* Practice on a scrap of fabric before painting on muslin angel.

EMBROIDERING: Back the angel with a layer of batting.

Outline-stitch every shape (*except* for the robe bands, stars, and the strings on the violin and bow), using floss colors slightly darker than the colors of the paint.

Couch down strands of gold metallic thread for the strings of the violin and bow.

For eyes and nose, work outline stitches using brown floss. Satin-stitch the mouth using pink.

APPLIQUÉING: Trace shapes for stars and robe bands from master pattern onto tissue paper; add ¼-inch seam allowances.

Cut shapes from blue calico and appliqué in place. Outline-stitch around shapes using blue pearl cotton floss.

ASSEMBLING: Cut angel from wood, adding 2 inches to pattern outline. Pad the wood with two layers of batting; mount angel over padded board, stapling excess fabric to back. Attach wire loop for hanging.

### For the ornaments

Use the pattern for the wall hanging, page 71, *actual size* for the ornament pattern. Add ⅜ inch around design, plus ¼ inch for seam allowances.

Trace the pattern onto tissue paper. Transfer to muslin, using dressmaker's carbon.

PAINTING AND EMBROIDERING: Paint and embroider ornaments in desired colors and as directed for wall hanging. *Note:* Use two strands of floss and one strand of metallic thread for em-

broidery. Work satin stitches on the stars. Embellish with beads.

ASSEMBLING: Lay painted angels atop lightweight fleece; sew along seamline. Cut out angels allowing ¼-inch seams. Cut same shape from muslin (backing).

Sew angel front to back, right sides facing, leaving an opening along the dress side. Clip seam every ⅛ inch. Turn and press.

Thread bobbin with medium metallic floss; use a lightweight metallic floss to thread top of machine. With the painted side of the angel toward the bobbin, stitch around the outside edge of the angel, except at opening, using a fine zigzag setting.

Stuff with fiberfill; sew opening. Zigzag-stitch over opening. Add ribbon loops for hanging.

# Cross-Stitched Ribbon-and-Lace Stocking

Shown on page 61.

Finished size is 15 inches tall.

## MATERIALS

⅓ yard *each* of hardanger (or 11-count Aida cloth), fleece, peach cotton fabric (backing), and ecru fabric (lining)
DMC embroidery floss in colors noted under color key
DMC gold metallic thread
1 package of gold crystal beads
1⅔ yards of ¼-inch-wide ecru lace (piping)
½ yard of 1¾-inch-wide pregathered ecru lace (cuff trim)
1 yard of ⅛-inch-wide peach satin ribbon
14 inches of ⅛-inch-wide pink satin ribbon
12 inches of ⅛-inch-wide pink lace
6 inches *each* of ⅝-inch-wide and ½-inch-wide ecru lace
Embroidery hoop and needle
Felt-tip markers
Graph paper
Water-soluble marking pen

## INSTRUCTIONS

### Charting the pattern

Make a full-color pattern for stocking and cuff. Using marking pens, transfer charts on pages 72 and 73 to graph paper, substituting colored Xs for symbols. Chart name on cuff, using the letters shown on chart for inspiration. Or substitute other alphabets.

### Preparing the materials

The stocking body measures approximately 9x15 inches. The cuff strip, excluding lace trim, is 4x14½ inches. Allow ½ inch for seams and enough fabric around both pieces of the stocking for placement in hoop.

*Note:* The cross-stitched portion of the stocking will have 5½ inches of *plain* fabric above it. Be *especially* careful to allow for this *before* beginning to stitch. The cross-stitched portion of the cuff is 4x7¼ inches and should be worked on the left-hand side of the cuff strip, allowing an additional 7¼ inches on the right side for the back of the cuff. Allow for seams.

Tape raw edges of fabric to prevent threads from raveling. Separate embroidery floss and use two strands for working cross-stitches. Use double strands of metallic thread.

Keep a record of the floss color numbers in case you need to purchase additional amounts.

*continued*

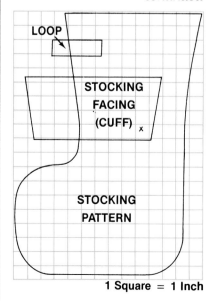

1 Square = 1 Inch

## Stitching the piece

Work stitches over two threads of fabric. Sew beads in place as marked on diagram.

Lace ⅛-inch-wide ribbons beneath gold stitches (noted by shaded areas on diagram)—pink, peach, then pink.

Sew ⅛-inch-wide pink lace in place (A on diagram). Use gold running stitches to sew ⅝-inch-wide and ½-inch-wide ecru lace atop pink lace (B and C on diagram). Sew beads or work peach French knots atop ecru lace to anchor in place (see photograph).

Remove tape. Press the piece.

## Assembling the stocking

Using the marking pen, draw cuff pattern onto stitched fabric to measure 4x14½ inches. Add a ½-inch seam allowance.

Draw stocking pattern onto the stitched fabric, using diagram as a guide. *Note:* You must count fabric threads to establish the stocking perimeter. Add 5 inches to stocking top. Add seams.

Zigzag-stitch along the cutting line *before* cutting out pattern pieces. This will prevent fabric from raveling.

Using the stocking front as a pattern, cut out two from fleece, one from backing fabric, and two from lining. Using cuff as a pattern, cut one from fleece, and one from lining fabric.

STOCKING: Stitch fleece pieces to wrong side of stocking front and back; trim fleece.

Sew the lining pieces together, right sides facing, leaving the top edge open. Trim seams and clip the curves.

Sew ¼-inch-wide ecru trim on seam line of stocking front. Sew front to back, right sides facing, leaving top edge open. Clip the curves, turn, and press.

CUFF: Sew fleece to wrong side of cuff. Fold cuff in half widthwise, right sides facing, and sew cuff seam. Repeat for the lining, omitting fleece. Sew ¼-inch-wide ecru trim to top of cuff.

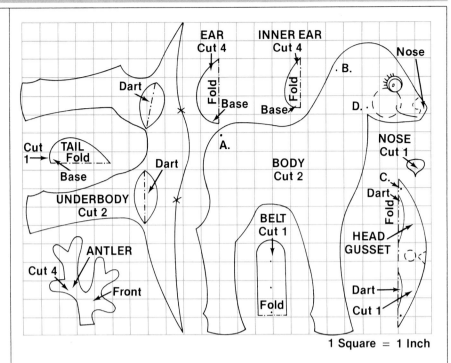

1 Square = 1 Inch

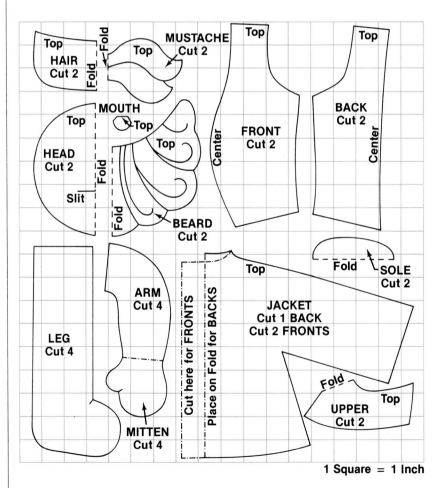

1 Square = 1 Inch

With right sides together, slip cuff over lining and sew bottom edge together. Trim seam, turn, and press.

STOCKING/CUFF ASSEMBLY: Insert cuff into stocking, *right* side of cuff facing *wrong* side of stocking top, matching cuff seam to left side seam of the stocking. Stitch cuff to stocking top. *Do not sew backing fabric into seam.* Trim seam.

Turn under seam on cuff lining; sew to seam of cuff top and stocking; press.

Turn cuff to outside of stocking. Sew 1¾-inch-wide lace to cuff edge. Weave ⅛-inch-wide peach ribbon through lace (or sew to top edge of lace), and tack a bow to side. Add loop for hanging.

# Advent Tree

Shown on page 63.

Finished size is 18½ inches tall.

## MATERIALS
1½ yards of green calico
⅔ yard of polyester fleece
2⅞ yards *each* of red piping,
   1¾-inch-wide white
   pregathered eyelet, and ⅜-
   inch-wide red dotted grosgrain
   ribbon
33½ inches of cable cord
One 10-inch-diameter circle of
   corrugated cardboard
Heavy string
Matching threads
Water-soluble marking pen
Fiberfill; kraft paper

## INSTRUCTIONS

TREE: Draw a 90-degree angle on kraft paper, extending lines for 20 inches. Connect these lines with a curved line, using a pencil-and-string compass. Add ¼ inch for seam allowances. This is the tree pattern.

Cut one tree from calico and one from fleece. Baste fleece to wrong side of calico.

POCKETS: From calico, cut out pockets with measurements as follow: 8x33½ inches (bottom pocket), 6½x26¼ inches, 6½x21 inches, 5½x14 inches, and 2½x8 inches (top pocket).

Cut one piece of piping, dotted ribbon, and eyelet for each pocket, using the longest measurement of each pocket. For the four lower pockets, baste piping to one long side of pocket. Fold pocket in half lengthwise, with right sides facing; sew long side together.

Turn pocket to right side and press. Pin dotted ribbon 1¾ inches from the pocket top.

For top pocket, omit piping and sew as directed for lower pockets. Pin dotted ribbon along pocket top, edges even.

For all pockets, sew top edge of ribbon in place. Place bound edge of eyelet under bottom ribbon edge; sew in place.

*continued*

1 Square = 4 Inches

# HOLIDAY TREATS FOR CHILDREN

**COLOR KEY**

| | | |
|---|---|---|
| ■ **Rose** | ⊠ **Dark Peach** | ▨ **Gold Metallic** |
| ■ **Green** | ⊡ **Light Peach** | ▨ **Green Half Cross-Stitches** |
| | ▢ **Pink** | ⊙ **Gold Beads** |

1 Square = 1 Cross Stitch

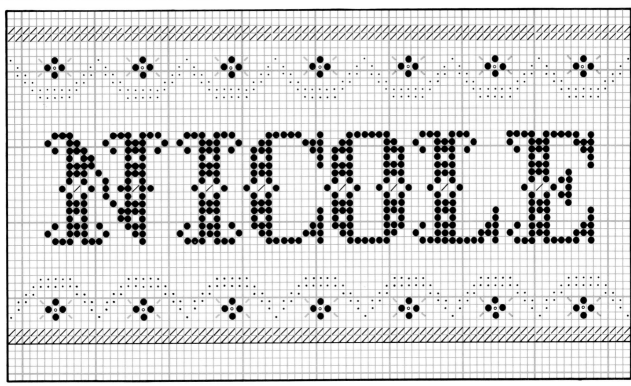

1 Square = 1 Inch

Divide strips for pockets, allowing for seams at ends. Use marker to mark dividers on *calico only.*

Sew longest pocket to tree bottom, leaving top edge open. Stitch dividers, beginning at the pocket bottom, and sew *under* eyelet to ribbon; sew from ribbon to top.

Repeat for other pockets, spacing them ½ inch apart. Sew dividers before stitching next pocket. (Top pocket has no dividers.)

TREE BASE: Cut a 5¾x33½-inch piece of calico (base). Cut a 1x33½-inch piece of calico (piping). For casing, sew short sides of base together for ¾ inch, skip next ½ inch for casing opening, then sew to end. At long edge nearest casing opening, press under ¼ inch and then press under ½ inch. Sew along bottom of casing; pull string through casing. For piping, cover cable cord with fabric. Sew piping to base.

### Assembling the tree
Fold tree in half, matching straight lines; sew this center back seam. Turn to right side.

Sew piped edge of base to bottom of tree. Stuff tree *firmly* with fiberfill; insert cardboard. Pull up string; tie. Trim tree as desired.

# Festive Skirt

Shown on page 62.

### MATERIALS
1 yard of green gingham fabric
Green, red, and yellow floss
¼-inch-wide elastic
DMC Cébélia crochet thread,
 Size 30: No. 666 red
Size 10 steel crochet hook

### INSTRUCTIONS

Use chart, *right,* for tree border. With two floss strands, work design along 45-inch-wide edge of fabric 4 to 6 inches from selvage. Repeat design along width.

Turn up a 4-inch hem. Measure desired length of skirt and turn under a 2½-inch casing at waist; fold under and topstitch.

Topstitch three parallel rows for two elastic casings, leaving openings. Topstitch along fold at waist. Insert elastic into casings; sew together. Sew openings.

### Crocheting the edging
Beg at long side make a chain slightly longer than the desired length of edging. *Row 1:* Sc in 6th ch from hook, * ch 3, sk 2 ch, sc in next ch. Rep from * across, ending with ch 1, dc in last ch, having number of lps divisible by 3, plus 2 more lps. Ch 3, turn.

*Row 2:* * Sc in next lp, ch 3. Rep from * across, ending with ch 1, dc in last lp. Ch 6, turn.

*Row 3: Sc in 4th ch from hook—*picot made; * ch 2, sc in next lp, ch 3, sc in next lp, ch 2, picot. Rep from * across. Break off.

Slip-stitch edging to the hem of the skirt.

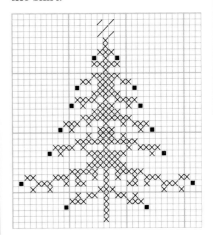

**COLOR KEY**   1 Square = 1 Stitch

▱ **Yellow**

⊠ **Green**

◾ **Red**

# CROCHETED GINGERBREAD HOUSE

Sweeter than sugar plums, this confectionery cottage will enchant young and old alike. Use it as a festive centerpiece, or turn it into a treasure box filled with candies, gifts, and other treats.

The sweater adaptation, *below,* is trimmed with a "front window" pocket and floral appliqués.

For instructions, turn the page.

# Crocheted Gingerbread House

## MATERIALS

DMC pearl cotton floss, Size 3:
  2 balls peach (754) for roof;
  2 balls coral (352) for roof;
  1 ball turquoise (807) for door
  and shutters; and 1 ball green
  (993) for flower boxes
DMC Cébélia crochet cotton,
  Size 10: 2 balls natural for
  house covering; and 1 ball
  *each* light pink (818), dark
  pink (3326), yellow (745),
  peach (754), green (913), dark
  green (320), beige (437),
  lavender (210), purple (208),
  and blue (799)
Brown embroidery floss
Steel crochet hooks Sizes 00, 4,
  and 8
1½ yards of muslin
Foam-core board or heavy
  cardboard (house)
Polyester batting (or fleece)

## INSTRUCTIONS

### House assembly

Each house section is assembled separately, then hand-sewn together to form the three-dimensional house shape.

Enlarge pattern, page 78, onto brown paper; cut out.

Cut one roof pattern from cardboard (or foam-core board) and one from batting; cut two from muslin, *adding 1-inch seams.* *Note:* Cut batting and cardboard pieces for roof in half along peak.

For house pattern, cut two *each* from cardboard (or foam-core board) and batting; cut four from muslin, *adding 1-inch seams.*

For the chimney, cut one shape from batting and two from muslin, adding 1-inch seam allowances to muslin pieces *only.*

For the house pattern pieces, make a tiny cut along the dot-dashed line (where a side meets either a front or back piece), for ease in turning outside corners.

For the bottom piece, cut two muslin rectangles measuring 9½x10½ inches (this includes ½-inch seams). Cut an 8½x9½-inch rectangle from cardboard. Do not cut a shape from batting.

Lay *one* muslin piece (for roof and house patterns) facedown on a working surface; place matching batting piece on top of corresponding muslin piece. Place cardboard piece on top of batting. Turn 1-inch seam allowances on muslin pieces to back side of cardboard pieces and glue to cardboard back; allow glue to dry.

Run a machine-stitched line between the two pieces where cardboard has been cut at top of roof. This allows the fabric to fold at the precise point where it turns corners.

Cover cardboard with matching muslin piece, turning all raw edges to the inside and tacking pieces in place along the edges of the main pattern pieces.

Assemble bottom piece as directed above, eliminating batting.

Slip-stitch house pieces together. Slip-stitch bottom piece to house section; set aside.

Assemble chimney by placing batting between muslin pieces. Turn raw edges to the inside and slip-stitch together. Sew chimney together along side; set aside.

### Crocheting

*Note:* All crochet pieces are smaller than the muslin house pieces. This is so the crochet fits the house snugly.

ROOF (make 2 pieces): With coral pearl cotton, Size 00 hook, ch 64.

*Row 1:* Dc in 4th ch from hook, * ch 2, sk 2 ch, dc in each of next 2 ch, rep from * across row—15 ch-2 sps made; ch 1, turn.

*Row 2* (right side): Sk 1st dc, sc in next dc; in next ch-2 sp work (sc, 2 dc, trc, 2 dc, sc); sc bet the next 2 dc; rep from * across row, ending with sc bet last dc and ch-3 lp and finishing last sc with peach; with peach, ch 2, turn. (Do not fasten off coral; leave at end and carry along side edges).

*Row 3:* Sc in 1st sc, * ch 2, sk scallop, in sc bet the 2 dc work (sc, ch 2, sc—ch-2 lp made); rep from * across row, ending with sc, ch 2, sc in last sc; ch 3, turn.

*Row 4:* In 1st ch-2 lp work (dc, sc); sc over next ch-2 lp behind the scallop; * in next ch-2 lp work (sc, 2 dc, trc, 2 dc, sc); sc over ch-2 lp behind scallop; rep from * across row; in last ch-2 lp work (sc, 2 dc), finishing last dc with coral; ch 2, turn. *Row 5:* Sc in 1st dc, ch 2, sk next 2 sts, * in sc over the ch-2 lp work (sc, ch 2, sc); ch 2, sk next scallop, rep from * across row, ending with ch 2, in top of ch-3 work (sc, ch 2, sc); ch 3, turn.

*Row 6:* Rep Row 4, end last dc with peach; ch 2, turn.

*Row 7:* Rep Row 5.

Rep Rows 4 and 5 until 19 rows of scallops completed, ending with Row 4, and continue to change colors every other row. Fasten off.

Make another side to correspond. Hand-sew two pieces together at center; pin assembled piece to roof and sew in place.

SCALLOPED STRIP TO FIT ALONG PEAK OF ROOF (make 2): With coral, ch 98. In 2nd ch from hook work (sc, 2 dc, trc, 2 dc, sc—finish last sc with peach). * Sk 2 ch, in next ch work (sc, 2 dc, trc, 2 dc, sc—finish last sc with coral); rep from * across row alternating the two colors. Fasten off. Pin and sew the strips to roof peaks. Set roof aside.

CHIMNEY: Use Size 8 steel hook, peach Cébélia, and coral pearl cotton. With peach, ch 60; join to make circle, being careful not to twist ch.

*Rnd 1:* Ch 3, dc in each ch around, join with sl st to top of ch-3 at beg of rnd.

*Rnds 2–6:* Ch 3. dc in each dc around; join to top of ch-3. *Rnd 7:* Ch 3, dc in next 29 dc, ch 3, turn—30 dc counting ch-3 as dc.

*Begin decrease for side—Row 8:* Work decrease over next 2 dc as follows: *yo, draw up lp in next dc, yo, draw thread through 2 lps on hook, yo, draw up lp in next dc, yo, draw through 2 lps on hook, yo, draw through rem 3 lps on hook—dec made.* Dc in next 25 dc, dec over next 2 dc; ch 3, turn.

*Rows 9–11:* Rep Row 8. Fasten off. Rep Rows 8–11 over rem stitches at end of Rnd 7.

With coral pearl cotton, work sc between each dc working *clock-*

*wise* around top of chimney piece. Slip finished piece over assembled chimney and sew in place, stretching to fit.

Stitch chimney to roof.

HOUSE COVERING: This piece is made in a long strip, joined to make a tube, slipped over the house, and then hand-sewn in place.

Use Size 8 hook and natural Cébélia thread: Ch 52.

*Row 1:* Dc in 6th ch from hook—to count as 2 dc and ch-1 sp; * ch 1, sk ch, dc in next ch; rep from * across row—24 ch-1 sps made. Ch 4, turn.

*Row 2:* Sk 1st dc, dc in next dc; * ch 1, dc in next dc; rep from * across row, ending with ch 1, dc in 5th ch of ch-6 at beg of Row 1; ch 4, turn. *Row 3:* Rep Row 2, except end row with dc in 3rd ch of turning ch-4. Rep Row 3 until piece measures about 35 inches. Sl st ends tog to make tube.

Slip tube over the assembled house, stretch and pin piece in place (do not sew). Mark four corner ch-1 sps at top of house with contrasting thread; remove tube. Marked threads should be about 27 to 28 rows apart across front and back of house.

*Row 1:* Join thread in one of the marked ch-1 sps (work across the shortest distance to the next marked ch-1 sp); ch 4, (dc over the next turning ch-lp, ch 1) 3 times; * dc in same st used for dc at end of row on the house tube, ch 1, (dc over the next turning ch-lp, ch 1) 4 times, rep from * across row to the next marked ch-1 sp— approximately 34 to 36 ch-1 sps across row.

*Row 2:* Ch 3, turn, *yo, draw up lp in 1st ch-1 sp, yo, draw through 2 lps on hook; yo, draw up lp in next ch-1 sp, yo, draw through 2 lps on hook, yo, draw through rem 3 lps on hook—dec made;* * ch 1, dc in next ch-1 sp, rep from * across row to last 2 ch-1 sps; work a dec in these 2 sps; ch 3, turn.

*Row 3:* Work dec over 1st 2 ch-1 sps, * ch 1, dc in next ch-1 sp, rep from * across row, end with dec over last ch-1 sp and top of ch-3 at end of row; ch 3, turn.

Rep Row 3 until one st rem. Fasten off. Repeat the triangular piece on the opposite end of the house between the rem 2 marked ch-1 sps.

GRASS AND TIMBER STRIPS: *Note:* Make 36-inch-long strip for grass using green. For timber, make two 36-inch strips, two 11-inch strips, four 3-inch strips, and six 1-inch strips using beige.

Use Size 8 steel crochet hook, green Cébélia (320) for grass, and beige Cébélia (437) for timber strips: Ch 5.

*Row 1:* In 5th ch from hook work *shell of 2 dc, ch 2, 2 dc;* ch 3, turn.

*Row 2:* Work shell in ch-2 sp of shell; ch 3, turn.

Rep Row 2 for required length for each strip.

*For grass only:* Working along one edge only, pivot work ch 3, sc in next turning ch-lp, * ch 3, sc in next turning ch-lp, rep from * across the strip, working sc in last turning ch lp. Fasten off. Attach strip to lower edge of house and hand-sew in place.

*For timber strips only:* Using photograph as guide, sew long strips to house, spacing 1 inch apart, stretching to fit. Sew 11-inch strips along triangular roof edges. Sew 4-inch strips on front and back of house as shown. Sew 1-inch strips evenly spaced vertically, on 2 sides of house between 2 long strips.

DOOR: Use Sizes 4 and 8 steel crochet hooks, and turquoise (807) and peach (754) pearl cotton: With turquoise and Size 4 hook, ch 26.

*Row 1:* Sc in 2nd ch from hook and in each ch across row; ch 1, turn.

*Row 2:* Working in *back loops,* work 2 sc in 1st sc, sc in rem sc across row; ch 1, turn.

*Row 3* (right side): Working under *both loops,* sc in each sc across row, ending 2 sc in last sc; ch 1, turn.

*Row 4:* Rep Row 2. *Row 5:* Rep Row 3. *Row 6:* Rep Row 2. *Row 7:* Rep Row 3.

*Row 8:* Working in *back loops,* dec over 1st 2 sc as follows: *Draw*

*up a lp in each of next 2 sc, yo, draw through 3 lps on hook—dec made.* Sc in each st across row, ch 1, turn. *Row 9:* Sc in each sc across, working dec over last 2 sc; ch 1, turn.

Rep Rows 8 and 9 two more times. Rep Row 8. Fasten off.

DOOR TRIM: With peach and Size 8 hook, right side facing, attach thread in bottom corner of door. Working around three sides of door, sc in each st around the two sides and work sc evenly spaced across the top of door; ch 1, turn.

Sl st in 1st sc, * in next sc work (hdc, dc, hdc), sl st in next sc; rep from * around. Fasten off.

DOOR HARDWARE TRIM: Using brown floss, work two sets of hinges by making straight stitch with three French knots.

Work six featherstitches with a French knot in the center for door hardware.

SMALL HEART FOR DOOR: Use Size 8 hook and Cébélia dark pink (3326): Ch 4.

*Row 1:* Work 2 dc in 4th ch from hook; ch 3, turn.

*Row 2:* Dc in 1st 2 dc, 2 dc in top of ch-3; ch 1, turn.

*Row 3:* Sc in 1st dc, 2 dc in next dc, sl st in next dc, 2 dc in next dc, sc in top of ch-3. Ch 1, pivot work, begin edging. Work sc, ch 1, evenly spaced around two sides of heart; join with sl st to sc at beg of Row 3. Fasten off. Sew to top of door.

LARGE HEART FOR ROOF PEAK: Use Size 8 hook and Cébélia dark pink (3326): Ch 4.

*Row 1:* Work 4 dc in 4th ch from hook; ch 3, turn.

*Row 2:* Dc in 1st dc and in each dc across row, 2 dc in top of ch-3; ch 3, turn.

*Row 3:* Rep Row 2; ch 1, turn.

*Row 4:* Sk 1st dc, * sc in next dc; in next dc work (dc, trc, dc), sc in next dc. Sl st in next dc. Rep from * once, ending with sl st in top of ch-3. Ch 1, pivot work and work edging as for small heart above. Fasten off. Sew to peak of roof.

*continued*

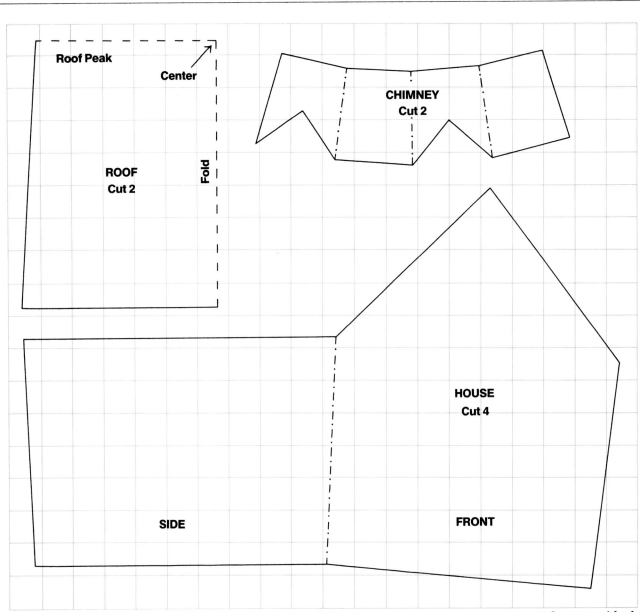

**Roof Peak**

**Center**

**ROOF**
**Cut 2**

**Fold**

**CHIMNEY**
**Cut 2**

**HOUSE**
**Cut 4**

**SIDE**

**FRONT**

**1 Square = 1 Inch**

MEDIUM WINDOW (make 2 for each side of door): Use Sizes 4 and 8 steel crochet hooks and Cébélia yellow (745) and peach (754), and pearl cotton turquoise (807). With yellow and Size 8 hook, ch 23. *Row 1:* Dc in 8th ch from hook; (ch 2, sk 2 ch, dc in next ch) 5 times; ch 5, turn.

*Rows 2-5:* Sk 1st dc, (dc in next dc, ch 2) 5 times; sk 2 ch of turning ch-5, dc in next ch; ch 5, turn. At end of Row 5, do not ch 5, do not turn.

*Row 6:* Pivot work, ch 2, dc in same ch as last dc; ch 2, dc in same ch used for dc in Row 3; ch 2, dc in same ch used for dc in Row 2; ch 2, dc in same ch used for dc in Row 1; ch 2, sl st in same

ch used for dc in foundation ch. Fasten off.

WINDOW TRIM: Join peach in right corner ch-2 sp at top of window, ch 1, work 2 sc in same sp; (in next ch-2 sp work sc, 3 dc, sc) 3 times; 2 sc in next ch-2 sp; continue around window working 3 sc around each turning-ch and 6 sc in the two corners. Join to sc at beg of rnd. Fasten off.

FIRST SHUTTER: With right side up and Size 4 hook, join turquoise in 4th sc of corner (in the 6 sc-group of the lower right corner), ch 1, sc in same st and in each of the next 18 sc; ch 1, turn.

*Row 2:* Working in *back loops,* work 2 sc in 1st sc, sc in back lp of rem sc across row; ch 1, turn.

*Row 3* (right side): Working under *both lps,* sc in each sc across row, ending 2 sc in last sc; ch 1, turn. *Row 4:* Rep Row 2. *Row 5:* Rep Row 3. *Row 6:* Rep Row 2. *Row 7:* Rep Row 3, do not increase in last sc. Fasten off.

SECOND SHUTTER: Join turquoise in 2nd sc in corner at top of window on other side; ch 1, sc in same st and in next 18 sc; ch 1, turn. *Row 2:* Sc in *back lp* of each sc across row and work 2 sc in last sc; ch 1, turn.

*Row 3:* Working under *both lps,* work 2 sc in 1st sc, sc in each sc across row; ch 1, turn. *Row 4:* Rep Row 2. *Row 5:* Rep Row 3. *Row 6:* Rep Row 2. *Row 7:* Rep Row 3, do not increase in 1st sc. Fasten off. Block; sew windows to house on each side of door.

SMALL WINDOWS FOR PEAK OF HOUSE (make 2): Use Sizes 4 and 8 steel hooks, Cébélia yellow (745) and peach (754); turquoise pearl cotton (807). With yellow and Size 8 hook, ch 14.

*Row 1:* Dc in 8th ch from hook; (ch 2, sk 2 ch, dc in next ch) twice; ch 5, turn.

*Row 2:* Sk 1st dc, dc in next dc, ch 2, dc in next dc, ch 2, sk 2 ch of turning-ch, dc in next ch; ch 5, turn.

*Row 3:* Rep Row 2. Do not ch 5, do not turn.

*Row 4:* Pivot work, ch 2, dc in same ch used for last dc, ch 2, dc in same st used for dc in Row 1, ch 2, sl st in same ch used for dc in foundation ch. Fasten off.

WINDOW TRIM: Join peach in right corner ch-2 sp at top of window; ch 1, 2 sc in same sp; in next ch-2 sp work (sc, 3 dc, sc); 2 sc in next ch-2 sp. Continue around window working 3 sc around each turning-ch and 6 sc in the two corner loops. Join to sc at beg of rnd. Fasten off.

FIRST SHUTTER: Work as shutter for medium window, except sc in next 10 sc instead of 18. Work five rows instead of seven. Fasten off.

SECOND SHUTTER: Work as shutter for the Medium Window except make changes to correspond with 1st shutter.

LARGE WINDOW (make 3 for each side and 1 for back): Use Sizes 4 and 8 steel hooks, Cébélia yellow (745) and peach (754), and turquoise pearl cotton (807): With yellow and Size 8 hook, ch 35. *Row 1:* Dc in 8th ch from hook; (ch 2, sk 2 ch, dc in next ch) 9 times; ch 5, turn.

*Rows 2–4:* Sk 1st dc, (dc in next dc, ch 2) 9 times; sk 2 ch of turning-ch, dc in next ch; ch 5, turn. At end of Row 4, ch 2, turn.

*Row 5:* Sk 1st dc, (dc in next dc, ch 2) 9 times; sk 2 ch of turning-ch. Sl st in next ch, ch 1, turn.

*Row 6:* Sl st in each of next 2 ch and next dc, ch 2, (dc in next dc, ch 2) 7 times; sl st in next dc. Fasten off.

WINDOW TRIM: Join peach in right ch-2 corner sp at top of window, ch 1, 2 sc in same sp, (in next ch-2 sp work sc, 3 dc, sc) 8 times, 2 sc in next sp. In each turning-ch and ch-2 sp around window, work 3 sc and at same time work 6 sc in each corner lp. Join to 1st sc at beg of rnd. Fasten off. Work 2 sc over each dc down the center strip of window. Fasten off.

Work shutters as for medium size window, except sc in next 12 sc instead of 18 sc. Work seven rows to complete shutters.

FLOWER BOXES (make 2 small, 2 medium, 3 large): Use Size 4 steel crochet hook, and green pearl cotton (993).

*Note:* Instructions are for the three sizes. Ch 10 for the small box; ch 17 for the medium box; and ch 27 for the large box.

Make required number of chains.

*Row 1* (right side): Dc in 4th ch from hook and in each ch across the row; ch 3, turn.

*Row 2:* Dc around post *from the back* of each dc across the row and the turning ch; ch 1, turn.

*Row 3:* Sc around post *from the back* of each dc across the row and the turning ch. Fasten off. Sew boxes to bottom edges of windows between the shutters.

FLOWERS (make 50 to 60): Use Size 8 steel crochet hook and assorted colors of Cébélia thread, Size 10. Ch 2, in 2nd ch from hook work sc, 2 dc, ch 2, sl st in same ch—petal made; * ch 2, in same ch used for 1st petal, work 2 dc, ch 2, sl st in same ch; rep from * 3 times more. Fasten off.

LEAVES (make 20 to 30): Use Size 8 steel crochet hook and Cébélia green (955). Ch 5, * sl st in 2nd ch from hook; sc in next ch, 3 dc in next ch, sl st in next ch—1 leaf made. Ch 7, rep from * for another leaf. Fasten off. Arrange flowers and leaves as desired in boxes and along grass; sew in place. Make French knots for flower centers.

**Final assembly**

Sew roof to house. (If house is used as a container, attach roof to house along one side only.)

# Crochet-Trimmed Child's Cardigan

### MATERIALS
Purchased cardigan
DMC Cébélia cotton thread, Size 10: scraps of light pink (818), dark pink (3326), yellow (745), peach (754), lavender (210), purple (208), and blue (799) for flowers; 1 ball green (913) for leaves and edging
DMC pearl cotton floss, Size 3: scraps of turquoise (807) for shutters, pale peach (754) for window edging, and dark peach (352) for flower box
Size 8 steel crochet hook
Lining fabric for pocket

### INSTRUCTIONS
Follow instructions for Grass Strips, page 77, to make three separate pieces for the sleeves and body.

*For pocket,* follow instructions for the Medium Window, Window Trim, First and Second Shutters, Flowers, and Leaves. *Note:* Crochet enough flowers and leaves to decorate the window box pocket and the grass edgings.

**To assemble**

*For edging:* Pin and stitch one edging around the body of the cardigan. Repeat for the sleeves.

Pin and slip-stitch the flowers and leaves in place.

*For the pocket:* Assemble the window pieces. Arrange flowers and leaves on the window box as desired; tack in place.

Cut a pocket lining, adding ¼-inch seams. Turn under seams and press. Sew lining to crocheted pocket, wrong sides facing. Sew pocket to cardigan front.

# ACKNOWLEDGMENTS

*We extend our sincere thanks and appreciation to each of the following talented people who contributed designs and projects to this book.*

Barbara Bergman—36 (place mats)
Taresia Boernke—34; 36 (guest towels); 59; cover and 63 (tree)
Chris Chennault—58
Coats & Clark—50 (gloves)
Laura Holtorf Collins—7 (heart ornaments); 48–51; 61
Phyllis Dunstan—12–13; 54–55
Pat Gaska—37
Nina Gordon—4–5
Becky Jerdee—35; 38 (tablecloth); 39 (barn picture)
Gail Kinkead—8–9
Jan Lewis—10–11
Genevieve Mason—7; 63 and cover (snowflakes)
Janet McCaffery—75 (house)
Jean Norman—30–33
Bonnie Schermerhorn—56
Shelley Thorton—60
Sara Jane Treinen—6; 75 (crocheted house)
Jim Williams—24–27; 57; 62

*For their courtesy and cooperation, we extend special thanks to:*

C.M. Offray & Son, Inc.
   261 Madison Ave.
   New York, NY 10016

DMC Corporation
   107 Trumbull Street
   Elizabeth, NJ 07206

Pendleton Woolen Mills
   489 5th Ave.
   New York, NY 10017

Plain n' Fancy, Inc.
   P.O. Box 756
   Jensen Beach, FL 33457

*We are also happy to acknowledge the following photographers, whose creative talents and technical skills contributed much to this book.*

Mike Dieter—24–25; 30–33; 35; 36 (guest towels); 48–49; 50 (detail)
Hedrich-Blessing—7 (snowflakes)
Hopkins Associates—4–5; 6–7 (angel, heart ornaments); 8–13; 26–27; 34; 36 (place mats); 50 (gloves); 51; 58–59; 60–61 (ornaments, stocking); 74–75
Mike Jensen—cover; 63
Scott Little—37–39
Bradley Olman—60 (angel wall hanging)
Perry Struse—54–57; 62